MW01681335

Grace

To Ruth & Vic,

Two dear and precious friends . . .

With great Love,

Joanne White Eagle

(April, 2013)

Copyright © 2012 by Jeanne White Eagle

All rights reserved. No other part of this book may be reproduced in any form or by any electronic or mechanical means including information storage and retrieval systems without permission in writing from the publisher, except by a reviewer, who may quote brief passages in a review. Published by Eltanin Publishing, 95 Spear St., Charlotte, Vermont 05445. First edition.

For more resources, visit http://www.eltaninpublishing.com/

ISBN: 978-0615721774 (Eltanin Publishing)

Edited by Catherine Ryan
Cover art and design by Joe Nusbaum

Grace

A Journey from
Betrayal to Healing

By
Jeanne White Eagle

Acclaim for Jeanne White Eagle's *Grace*

Grace is a story with lessons for everyone who has ever been hurt or felt betrayed at some time in their lives. And who hasn't? The author shares her personal experience both as a witness to emotional scars in others as well as her own story and her process of forgiveness. Compelling and inspiring.

—John Renesch, Global Futurist

The book will have great appeal to anyone who WANTS to heal a broken relationship and has tried and seems to get stuck. I think that many of us have been in that situation, where we've prayed and prayed, and seemingly nothing was happening.

— Pat Joynes, Editor

Jeanne's voice is dramatic; she knows how to set a scene. There is no doubt she is the harried heroine of this story, as she should be. It is to Jeanne's credit that she pursues her questions with spiritual fervor. Her perception of betrayal, as harsh as it was, also serves as a goad to her dawning realization that "always the way is open to you to choose Love. Always there is a way to see beauty and Light even when it appears darkness is unfolding. See the darkness as the doorway to Light."

— Tom Bissinger, Author & Playwright

Dedicated to

my children Jenny and John Troutner
my beloved husband, John Pehrson
and to my parents, Kit and Bill,
who helped me to believe and trust in myself and follow my dreams.

Contents

Foreword
Laying the Foundation

FIRST STORY

Part I: Bosnia

Chapter 1 — Precipice 7
Chapter 2 — Emsuda 11
Chapter 3 — Friends 15
Chapter 4 — War's Legacy 17

SECOND STORY

Part II: Setting the Stage

Chapter 5 — Threshing Floor 25

Part III: Dance

Chapter 6 — Seeds 31
Chapter 7 — Beginnings 33
Chapter 8 — Invitations 37
Chapter 9 — Vision 39
Chapter 10 — A Singing Dance 41
Chapter 11 — Dance Prep 43
Chapter 12 — Changes 45
Chapter 13 — Angel 49
Chapter 14 — Rain 51

Part IV: Betrayal

Chapter 15 — Face of Fear 57
— Friday 58
— Saturday Morning 59

Chapter 16 — Saturday Afternoon 61

Part V: Crucible
Chapter 17 — Flight 71
Chapter 18 — Dream 73
Chapter 19 — Diving Hand 77
Chapter 20 — Saibaba 81
Chapter 21 — Anger? 83
Chapter 22 — Stuck in Form 87
Chapter 23 — Waking Up 89
Chapter 24 — Challenged 91
Chapter 25 — More Dreams 95
Chapter 26 — Echoes 97
Chapter 27 — Walking Through Gardens 101

Part VI: Grace
Chapter 28 — Insights 107
Chapter 29 — Forgiveness 109
Chapter 30 — Love 111
Chapter 31 — Reaching Out 113
Chapter 32 — Heaven 117
Chapter 33 — Heart Dance 119
Chapter 34 — Wings of Angels 123
Chapter 35 — Realization 127
Chapter 36 — Keeping Time 131
Chapter 37 — Suspension 133
Chapter 38 — Trust 137
Chapter 39 — Memory 139
Chapter 40 — Grace 141

Part VII: Coming Full Circle
Chapter 41 — Resolve 149

Part VIII: Epilogue
Epilogue 157
Acknowledgements 161
About the Author 163

GRACE

"...an unmerited divine assistance
given humans for their regeneration
or sanctification; a virtue coming from God."

— Merriam-Webster Collegiate Dictionary

Foreword

Since we are living at a time of major global transformation, it is both important and useful to have accounts — real-life accounts — that illustrate the spiritual journey. It is even more useful when such accounts come along with multiple spiritual lessons that illustrate the value of questioning and seeking with an attitude of openness and humility. Such an account is Grace.

As the title implies, Jeanne White Eagle was gifted or "graced" with the answer to a question that arose from her experiences in Bosnia in 2007. Multiple people recounted to her their experiences in the war that followed the break-up of Yugoslavia in the 1990's. The horror of these stories led Jeanne to wonder how such atrocities can happen: What is it that leads people to commit heinous acts against neighbors and even friends? Jeanne prayed repeatedly for insights about this. And her prayers were answered.

Which presents one of the spiritual lessons in *Grace*: "Be careful what you ask for, for you might just get it!" So goes the old adage. But often the request is fulfilled in a way we don't expect. Rarely are we able to comprehend the mind of God, or to recognize the depth of questions we pose to the Universe. Many times our answer comes not in words but in a life experience that offers us an all-too-personal taste of the essence of our question.

In Jeanne's situation she was mystified as to how friends and neighbors could betray each other and her answered prayer showed up in just that way — in an unexpected personal experience. Jeanne's account of this experience shows how richly the Universe will answer our requests, providing not just insights but opportunities for our growth.

Grace also takes up the question of why people do what they do, revealing how fear and ego so often lie at the base of human motivation. In this regard, one of the great merits of *Grace* is its illustration of the power of love, compassion and humility to transcend pride and transform fear. As you will discover as you read Jeanne's story, it was neither easy nor pleasant for Jeanne White Eagle to summon the courage and trust in Spirit that were required for her to return love for fear and humility in place of an ego stuck in form.

What does it mean "to get stuck in form"? This is a third key spiritual lesson that *Grace* offers us. The various wisdom literatures of all cultures tell us that the Divine "makes all things new." (Rev. 21:5) In living systems change is the norm, an ecological fact, an omnipresent feature of reality. Yet we humans find change difficult.

We don't want to give up familiar ways of thinking. We don't want to let go of old ways of acting. We'll find ourselves saying "But I/we've always done it this way!" Or we hang on to habits that exclude rather than include, e.g. attitudes and mind-sets that push away those who aren't of our tribe, our religion, our denomination, our nationality etc. These patterns of thinking and acting are "forms" that hamper our moving into the new reality being offered to us by the Divine. Jeanne White Eagle's story illustrates what it looks like, in modern real-life situations, when people get stuck in form, and the unfortunate, spiritually-destructive consequences that can result.

Because ours is a transitional time, moving as we are from the Age of Pisces to the Age of Aquarius, at the end of one Mayan baktun and the beginning of another, change is coming at us on all fronts, at a pace faster all the time. Now more than ever we cannot afford to get stuck in form. We must not resist the new.

How we might handle ego, find courage within and develop trust in the Divine — these are some of the vital lessons in Jeanne's story. It is a deeply personal story that is at the same time universally applicable to anyone on the journey to Spirit.

Susan Mehrtens, Ph.D.
President, Jungian Center for the Spiritual Sciences
Waterbury, Vermont
October 2012

Grace

Laying the Foundation

Someone once said, "Don't ever begin with an apology."

Whoever that person was couldn't have been raised in the South. In Tennessee, you're taught straight out of the birth canal to say, "Yes ma'am." "No ma'am." "Yes sir." "No sir." "Thank you." And in every other sentence, "I'm sorry." So here I go, right from the start, giving you an apology from an ole Tennessee girl. I am not a writer. At least not by any good author's standing. And so for this I ask the reader's forgiveness. I do, however, have a story to tell. Actually, I have two stories, each of which intertwines in such a way that it is impossible for me not to share them in the same telling.

In 2007 my husband John and I went to Bosnia. It was our first visit. Nothing could have prepared either of us for our experience there, for the stories we were told, for the remnants of destruction we saw left from a war that ended years ago in 1995. We were only there a few days, yet in those few days we were exposed to a reality that drove me to ask over and over again, "How? How can human beings do this to each other?" How do people who have grown up side by side as neighbors, lifelong family friends, friends who have helped to build each other's houses, schools, mosques, churches… how can they turn on each other in what seemed to be in the blink of an eye, sowing a seed of evil so devastating that even now the brokenness is as evident as if the war was yesterday!?

And then, once all is said and done, how does one heal? How do relationships heal? How, when all has been broken apart, cruelly and methodically, does the human psyche find wholeness again? Is it even possible?

The first story began in Bosnia… a second-hand account which quickly found its way into a first-hand experience.

The second story is a personal one of unexpected twists and turns. Buried within it are the answers I sought to the questions arising from the first story. *How* can such horror happen? And then *how* does the healing occur? More to the point, *can* healing occur?

Some of the names and dates used throughout have been changed. This is done mostly to honor the privacy of certain individuals and the confidentiality of circumstances. Other names have not been changed. This is to honor those without whom certain extraordinary events (miracles?) couldn't have taken place.

Jeanne White Eagle
November, 2009

FIRST STORY

Part I

BOSNIA

Of the nine levels of hell,
the lowest and most severe
is the Betrayal of Trust

— Dante

Chapter 1

Precipice

One was a Muslim. One was a Serb. The first, a student. The second, his teacher. I didn't actually know them. But I did meet them once. In a vision. It was in a ceremonial dance, a sacred medicine dance. We were dancing in Ireland. I had gone more than 24 hours with no food. No water. And then without warning, I fell to the ground. And there they were. Arms over each other's shoulders, saying to me, "We will help you." Now, even as I write this, I feel them next to me… helping me to write it as it was. As it happened.

It was in 2005. A close friend said, "You have to go to Bosnia." She herself is from Croatia. She had come to Germany to join us in a ceremonial dance there, having spent the last days at a conference in Sarajevo. It was here that she met a beautiful and courageous woman named Emsuda.

Emsuda was Bosnian… a Muslim who came from a small village that was destroyed during the Bosnian war. When our friend first spoke of the woman, I got this peculiar feeling in my belly. I knew one day I would meet her. Two years later, our paths finally crossed.

We went to Bosnia twelve years after the war had ended. The purpose was to meet the people and let them meet us. Because of certain political mishaps during the war, Americans were often seen with suspicion and mistrust. If we had any hope of coming here in the future, it was important that the people meet us, to see that we had no political or religious agenda. With the help of friends, my husband John and I introduced ourselves through an informal concert in the town of Viseko near Sarajevo. There we fell in love with these extraordinary people. It was clear, right from the beginning that those in this part of the world were tender, beautiful and with all they'd been through, were still so willing to open their hearts and homes to us.

What I began to see early on, however, was the brokenness in many of those we met, particularly in the men. And after further observation I saw a sadness in both men and women that didn't show itself in the first minutes of our meeting. What brought this to my awareness in a jolt was a meek middle-aged woman who, after the concert, stayed discreetly at my side as I moved among the people. Finally, I turned to her and smiled. It was then she asked in a quiet voice, "Please, may I continue to stand next to you? You are full of so much joy." My eyes filled with tears as it began to dawn on me that I was standing at the precipice of something I wasn't sure I had the courage to pursue.

In the next days, we learned that every person we met had a story. Most were heartbreaking stories, telling of the brutal tortures and horrendous murders of family members and neighbors. As I listened, I found that even with the experience John and I have had in so many other parts of the world, where we have found ourselves inside war-torn countries and communities in deep conflict, we had not known the depth of horror that was possible until now.

Who's to say that one evil is more horrible than another when compared to the atrocities of Hitler, Stalin, the Spanish Inquisition, and so on? What I do know is that, in my experience, there is no comparison with one evil to another when the soul of a person is being methodically ripped apart by another, particularly another in whom one has loved and trusted as a friend or relative.

We listened to story after story. When it seemed our time in Bosnia was coming to an end, I wondered if there might be a way to connect with Emsuda. I asked our Croatian friend who had met Emsuda in Sarajevo two years before. After a couple of telephone calls, it was done. We were on our way to a small village in the Northwest of Bosnia.

Chapter 2

Emsuda

When we arrived, I was touched by the simplicity and beauty of this village. Immediately, I saw a mosque and very near to it, a Serbian orthodox church. There were cafes, coffee shops, small markets of fresh fruits and vegetables. Children were running up and down the sidewalks. The town's people were involved in their everyday lives. It all seemed pleasant enough.

What I didn't learn until later is that this village, once inhabited by more than twenty thousand people, had been completely destroyed in the war. The Serbian army rounded up row upon row of men (mostly Muslim) between the ages of eighteen and sixty-five, lined them up and shot them. Trucks would move down the streets and gather up truckloads of young people, take them into the nearby forests and shoot them… creating mass graves that are still there today. When most of the men and young people were destroyed, the remaining women and children were rounded up, taken to concentration camps where the women were tortured and raped. It was inside this horrific chaos, that all buildings (houses, churches, schools, businesses) were burned. All… burned to the ground until nothing remained but ashes.

This was a scenario that was being repeated time and time again throughout that part of the world during the war. Whatever sinister political games were being played by politicians worldwide at the time, the result was a playing field that invited the cruelest and most evil possibilities man can create.

As we drove through this village, now rebuilt and alive again, we pulled into the driveway of an impressive multi-storied white building that had a sign on the outside that said "House of Peace." We walked inside and were welcomed warmly by the staff.

Soon, Emsuda appeared. What a striking soul! Medium build, dark blond hair, deep eyes that glowed with warmth and kindness. She spoke no English, and I, no Bosnian. So we were very grateful for the competent translation offered by our traveling companions.

During the next hours and on into the next day, Emsuda shared her journey over the years during the war and after. It was not an easy one. When her village was destroyed, along with many of her friends and family, she was one of those women taken to the concentration camps.

After the war, miraculously having survived the camps, Emsuda and other women from the village returned to what had once been their homes. With their brooms, they began to sweep and clean the streets, preparing the land for new life. It is hard to imagine the courage and the stamina it must have taken to return to this site where so much pain had taken place, committing to begin again. It was during this period of time that Emsuda had a vision… a dream to build a "House of Peace" where those, particularly women, who had lost so much… their husbands, brothers, fathers, mothers, sons and daughters… could grieve, heal and begin anew.

And so, with the help of many from England and other countries, mostly women who somehow had learned about the project, the building in which we stood was built from the love donations that came in from all over the world.

One of the projects Emsuda and the House of Peace were presently working on at the time of our visit involved an entire wall that was to be covered with photographs of those brutally killed when the village was destroyed.

As we were listening to Emsuda tell the stories of her village, one woman walked in with photographs of her son and husband, both gone, leaving her alone during these years since the war. As she handed the photos to Emsuda, she began to cry. As she did, I felt my own tears. The project of the photographs was to put all of them on a large wall so that those in the photos could look down to see that their wives, mothers, sisters and daughters not only survived but were moving on with their lives, finding joy again. This was a very brave and positive project. And as we observed and listened, I was becoming more and more aware of the strength and courage it took for these women to move beyond the fear they had known so intimately.

It was when our small group created a song for Emsuda as a parting gift of gratitude, that she, with moist eyes, quietly got up from her seat and walked to a table where there lay a large pile of photographs. She returned to her seat, and it was then that she shared some of the truly heartbreaking stories. This was when I first heard the story of the coach and the student.

Chapter 3

Friends

Emsuda pulled out a photograph of a young man who looked to be in his early twenties. He had been an athlete, a wrestler, who showed great promise. So much so, that his coach chose to train him as a champion. And this he became. A champion competitor who won awards and accolades for his extraordinary ability. Through the years, the student (a Muslim) and the coach (a Serb) became close friends. Their families shared meals together. They all took pride in being part of a close community where one might hear proud comments from a Serb who helped to build a neighboring mosque, "that is *my* mosque." Or you might hear a Muslim say of a church he or she had helped to build, "that is *my* church." This was the environment that nurtured the friendship of the student and the coach, a friendship that promised to last, perhaps, a lifetime.

Then the war happened. Something changed. Almost overnight a fear took root, a hate so dark that one wonders that light had ever shown in this land that had known so much warmth and possibility. Neighbor turned on neighbor, friend upon friend.

And so it happened that the coach, now a Serbian soldier, was part of a force that was hell-bent on bringing genocide to all Muslims and Croats who crossed their paths. Thus, into this village where families were nurtured and differences were honored, war came.

The student was taken prisoner. The coach, knowing the student, was given the responsibility of torturing the student. Bit by bit, the coach cut away the flesh of his one-time friend, a friend he had played with, eaten with, come to love as his own family. Slowly, methodically, amidst the screams of pain and agony that defy the imagination, the body of this student was cut and dissected until he finally died.

How? How was this possible? When I heard this story, my stomach turned. The flood of tears I felt wouldn't come because they were blocked by *shock* in hearing that such a betrayal could happen. And I just kept asking myself, how? How?

Chapter 4

War's Legacy

I've heard so many stories over the years… met souls who have suffered severe torturous heartbreaking circumstances… Jews who survived the holocaust in Germany, Palestinians who have had everything taken from them, black South Africans who carry the memories of the harsh and brutal era of Apartheid, children of many countries suffering from unimaginable abuses… so many stories, so many lives that have known the deepest meaning of pain.

Perhaps it was the timing… the circumstances… I don't know. I do know that this whole experience in Bosnia was a pivotal time for me. It was *this* story… this one story of the student and his coach which was to haunt me for many months afterward. Even a year after meeting the people, hearing the stories, seeing the gunshot and mortal impact scars still so prevalent throughout our visit, I found I could barely speak of our experiences, the pain was so great.

And the questions were ongoing, pestering unknowns, *how? How can this happen?* What is it that occurs inside the human psyche that brings our own species to the point of destroying itself so utterly, with such malice and hate?

And then what happens after? After the war? Emsuda shared that once they began rebuilding their village, people started to return. Astoundingly, this included not only those who had received torture and suffering from the hands of those who inflicted pain, but it also included those who had committed these heinous crimes.

For instance, a woman who had lost her husband at the gunpoint of a neighbor turned soldier, might be walking down the street and find the same soldier walking on the opposite sidewalk on the same street. Or they might see each other in a food market, or a café.

How surreal is this? How does one continue and stay in integrity with one's heart when the perpetrator and those whom he might have tortured, come face to face on a daily basis?

I did notice that those who were at the receiving end of the criminal abuses, if they didn't have access to someone such as Emsuda and her House of Peace, were more often than not, trapped in a role of "not dealing" with the hurt. Rather, they were doing the best they could to live as though nothing had happened. This was overwhelmingly difficult for those who had lost family members or were somehow themselves impaired from the abuse.

In turn, so many of those who had committed the crimes, once having returned to what they knew before the war, were broken. Broken souls, often having done things in the war they would never have conceived possible of themselves. Perhaps this is the way it always is in war.

What happens then on the other side of the act itself?... *How* does the *healing* take place? *Can* healing occur? Is it even possible for relationships to heal, a community to heal, a country, when the trust has been so purely, so profoundly broken? When *betrayal* is the dragon that rears its head? When the relationship of friends, neighbors, has been blasted apart unexpectedly, instantly, and so completely? *How does the healing happen?*

Some would say "forgiveness" is the way to healing. But you know what? *Forgiveness* is simply a word that is no more than an intellectual concept if there is still anger in the heart. One can say "I forgive" all day long, but it has no meaning if a person can't get to a place of total resolve with one's *feelings* around the issue at hand.

Thus, I found myself praying, *every day, several times a day,* two prayers. First, how is such horror, such betrayal, such abuse as we had seen, possible? And second, how do the relationships heal, both for one's self and for all others involved?

It wasn't long before I got my answers.

Now begins the second story.

SECOND STORY

Part II

SETTING THE STAGE

"One does not become enlightened by imagining figures of light but by making the darkness conscious. The latter procedure, however, is disagreeable and therefore unpopular."

— C.G. Jung

"Know that Life continues to move in the direction of Love… Even when it seems to be moving away from it."

— from Journal of Jeanne White Eagle

Chapter 5

Threshing Floor

To begin the story that follows in these next pages, it is important to say that I in no way have gone through, at any time in my life, the horrors that have been inflicted on those in war. What I can say is that, over a prolonged period of time, I have been with those who have had the unfortunate circumstance of having lived through such an experience. And I have come to an appreciation of the torment that for so many is still very much alive today, regardless of the fact that the conflict itself may have long since ended.

Over the last decades I have also had the opportunity of working with persons, particularly youth, who have survived horrific abusive environments. Though I have no formal scholastic degree in such areas, I do have life experience and the willingness to reach out when the need has arisen.

My life experience has brought me to a place that has allowed me to appreciate and more fully understand that though a set of circumstances may deeply influence the choices one might make in life, it is finally the *will* that lies within each of us that determines what direction we eventually end up taking. I have seen a young person, beaten within inches of his life, *make a conscious choice* not to inflict the same behavior onto another. I have seen a woman, whose husband was brutally murdered in an act of war, *make a conscious choice* to come from forgiveness rather than vengeance. Some might argue that it is not *will* but the belief that we each have a *destiny* that determines our direction. But even here, it is through our *will* that we determine which choices we make and that, one way or the other, brings about the fulfilling of one's destiny.

So, what happens if the *will* is broken? Can the *will* be broken?

The story I share in the next pages cannot be compared to the one just given regarding Bosnia, not in the sense of shared *physical* hurt and pain. I have never been raped. I have never been tortured, certainly not in the way or to the extent described in previous pages. Nor have I ever been broken, not to the degree that we saw in Bosnia, particularly in the Serbian men.

It is on the threshing floor of the *psyche* that I have come face to face with my own personal inferno. This is where the wounds made upon the soul from the imprint left from an abuser's hand cannot be measured en masse, but only through the individual's response to an experience that for her or him manifests pure trauma and perhaps terror.

The open and raw wounds of the psyche, then, can often reap scars that are far deeper and longer lasting than those that are physically induced. This I have seen others experience, some of whom after decades have never found healing or resolve. This I have had the opportunity to experience in my own personal journey, though in a different context, with different results.

I had prayed for answers. Answers to the how and why something as what occurred in Bosnia could possibly take place. My prayer was answered. But not in a way that anyone could have anticipated.

Though the depth may not measure up to that of those who have filled a lifetime with unresolved pain, nonetheless, the story that follows in the next pages carries the seeds of trauma that leave the possibility of permanent scars. Except by conscious choice that gave fertile ground to what some would say happened "by the Grace of God," I might still be locked inside a prison of spiraling emotional upheaval.

Part III

DANCE

"No one places her dreams in the hands of those who might destroy them."

— Paul Coelho
from "Witch of Portobello"

Chapter 6

Seeds

A story has many beginnings. The challenge is to choose the one that communicates the intent of the telling in the moment a story is told. And so…

A few years ago in a small town in the countryside of rural America, I experienced one of the most devastatingly emotional traumas of my life. It isn't that this was the only time in my life where I've experienced chaotic and transformative events. And it certainly isn't to be compared with anyone else's own experiences of deep trauma. It's that this particular experience was so unexpected, so shocking and painful, that any description of an emotional hell couldn't have been more horrific and heartbreaking than this was to me. Yet… it carried within it the seeds that would help me grow to an understanding of the questions that had haunted me since our time in Bosnia.

It feels important to say that as I share my story with you, the reader, I do so with the full awareness that each person's life experience is personal and subjective. To walk in another's moccasins, borrowing from Native wisdom, is a beautiful sentiment but the reality is that no one can fully understand, particularly at the cellular level, what a person may have experienced in his or her life given a certain set of circumstances. I can surmise what you might have endured at some point in your life. I can even have a deep appreciation and perhaps an inkling of understanding, but try as I might, I cannot fully know the truth of an experience for you because it is not my experience. It is yours, unique unto you.

What I give to you now in the following pages is my own personal experience of what occurred months later after our return home from Bosnia..

Out of this experience answers would come… answers I already intuited, intellectually knew, but had no way of bridging the chasm between the knowing and the actual freedom from the emotional chains such pain can produce. I would describe it as an *imprisoning of the soul's heart.*

Chapter 7

Beginnings

John and I traveled very different journeys to find each other. Our childhoods couldn't have been in more contrasting circumstances.

His early years were sprinkled with not-so-happy memories of an unsettled family life which included long periods of separation from his mother due to an illness that took her away for months at a time. His father's inability to raise his young son resulted in fragmented experiences of living with relatives and eventually, foster parents. The crowning touch of childhood for John found him living out his teen years on a boy's farm where to be the toughest meant survival. He was the toughest.

I, on the other hand, was raised in a true Ozzie and Harriet environment, but with considerable more depth I might add. My father, an engineer, spent hours teaching my brother, sister and me about the physics of our world through creative and wonderful inventions and experiments. At the same time, his innate ability to create a safe and loving space infused with wisdom far beyond his years, became the well from which I would drink for many years to come. And my mother? She was and is a shining light in my life. Always she, along with my dad, has been there for me, encouraging me when I most needed it and helping me to pick myself up when I would fall. Clearly my upbringing was infused with genuine parental love and guidance that most people, as I've learned over the years, only dream of. In short, my parents instilled in me the belief that I could do anything, that nothing was impossible as long as I put my heart and mind into it.

The years that followed childhood were filled with a menagerie of life's colorful opportunities. Receiving University degrees, John and I each went on to pursue wherever our dreams were leading us at the time. This included a number of relationships, marriages, divorces, and gratefully, the glorious creation of children.

I entered the corporate world while in my thirties. John had already been in the business environment for some twenty plus years. We didn't know it then, but our paths were destined to cross in this arena.

Our coming together happened at a time in our lives when it was apparent that all that had occurred up to that point was to specifically prepare us for the journey we would soon be embarking upon together. Maybe this is the way it is for everybody. For us it became clear as crystal. We were in our mid-forties at the time.

We met through an organization called the World Business Academy made up of executives from around the world who were concerned about the state of our planet and who were willing to assume responsibility for the direction in which it was going. After many years of involvement in the business world, and as a result of serendipitous events that brought us into contact with such teachers as India's Satya Sai Baba and Native American Joseph Rael, our lives took a one hundred eighty degree turn.

We came to the realization that if one person can make a difference in the world, then two people surely can. We left the corporate world. Quickly, we found ourselves walking a path that demanded full surrender and the eventual letting go of all that previously would have represented security for us. We gave away most of what we had, including letting go of our home to now travel the world doing workshops on conflict resolution and other related topics, peace concerts, and ceremonial dances. All was very unconventional and certainly not recognized as credible by a more well-established traditional mainstream audience. It didn't matter. We had made our choice. If there is such a thing as *destiny* then it was clear that we were being pulled onto its path.

Chapter 8

Invitation

In the late 90s, John and I were invited to come to the land of two very dear friends, whom I will call Jonas and Sarah. We loved going there. We were always warmly received and found many opportunities to interact in fun and creative ways. Over the years that followed, more and more people were becoming part of their community and it was exciting to watch it grow and flourish. It wasn't a "live in" community where others lived on the land. But it was a place where people were drawn to the activities and the nurturing energy of the land and people, often coming long distances. Here they found something that fed their souls. Because of John's and my growing commitments around the world, there was little time and resources to have a home of our own. Therefore, when we were in the States, we naturally felt a much-needed sense of "home" with Jonas, Sarah and the community that was growing around them. As a result, we often based out of that part of the country.

The people there became our dear and trusted friends. They were becoming *family*. There was a great sense of love and genuine caring, and when we were able to be with them, we experienced the meaning of true community. It didn't take much to see first-hand how a peaceful world was possible if people cared for each other in the authentic way these people did.

We felt so welcomed and loved here that whenever John and I would dream about the day we could settle down and once again have a permanent place to call home, we would think of Jonas, Sarah and the community around them.

Then something changed.

Chapter 9

Vision

When I received the vision for a ceremonial singing dance in 1996, a Native American friend and mentor shared, *"If you've had a vision and it is a true vision, once it starts to take off, all you can do is hold on for dear life."* And this is exactly what happened.

It took seven years for this vision to gestate and for me to find the courage to say or do anything about it. It was only when I mentioned it to this Native friend that, with his encouragement, I stepped off the cliff into an unknown space with no guarantee of the outcome, and found to my amazement that the vision I had been given so many years before, indeed, was a true vision. It took off like a kite in a huge wind and flew.

So what is a ceremonial dance? It is a dance that is done in a sacred way. There are many different kinds of ceremonial dances, the majority of which have been done for centuries by various indigenous peoples all over our planet. And all of them, in one way or another, have a sacred purpose and relate to a spiritual belief of some sort. We see this in the Native American, Mayan, African, Australian Aborigine cultures and so many more.

It is safe to say that each ceremonial dance in its own uniqueness, serves the people. *The people* can be defined as each and every form of life on this planet and beyond. The purpose of the dance I was given is to provide a loving space that focuses on clearing and healing whatever is within a person that keeps that person from realizing his or her full potential. In other words, it helps that person to remove whatever it is that separates her or him from God or Love.

It is a dance that can produce visions, and at the same time help one process through issues of hurt, pain, anger, rage, etc. It is a dance that serves the whole. Many ceremonial dances may focus on the *external* which may have internal shifts and changes, where other dances may focus on the *internal* which may manifest external shifts and changes. We call this latter a *medicine dance.*

Whatever form a dance has taken, if done in a good way, it brings the opportunity for transformation to the life of an individual as well as that of the mass consciousness for generations to come.

The dance for which I had been given a vision was a *medicine dance.*

Chapter 10

A Singing Dance

It was in January 2003 that my husband John and I went to visit our dear Native friend and teacher. It was here, in one quiet moment during our visit that I shared with him the vision I had received seven years before of a singing dance. Again, I had not said anything about it until now, mostly from lack of courage. In a quiet voice he said, "It's time."

The first dance occurred that following spring in the United States. From there it spread quickly around the world. The first country to invite the dance from outside the USA was South Africa. After South Africa came Israel. From there the dance moved into Europe, then the Balkans, and South America.

Some months later the first of the *youth dances* took place. It was for a group of young people, each of whom had been highly abused, sexually and otherwise, most since birth. The invitation itself came from two dear friends, one a *movement therapist*, the other a *medical doctor* who specializes in neurological disorders. These two extraordinary people had the unique and heavy responsibility of working with some of the more severely abused children in our present day society. After having experienced the dance themselves, they decided this singing dance would be a particularly effective vehicle to help these children process and heal from hurts that might otherwise stay with them for life. The whole experience turned out to be extremely powerful for these young dancers.

Something unexpected happened, though. As the dance moved through the first hours and into the next day with the young dancers singing and processing the angers and hurts they had undergone in their young years, John and I saw something we didn't anticipate. *The crew was also processing.* Big time!

None of us foresaw the depth of the impact the young people's dancing and singing through their hurts, would have on the crew. Many of the adults who had unresolved issues from childhood began to process during the dance as well, along with the youth dancers. By the end of the dance itself, the crew was exhausted. The dance had begun Friday afternoon and ended on Sunday morning. This included rest periods in the day and night times.

Luckily, there were enough on the crew who were able to remain centered and who could capably and lovingly care for the young dancers throughout. But this experience was an important lesson to remember as we moved forward with the *youth dances.* It was after this experience, that we became more astute and aware of who would crew the *youth dances* from that point on.

Chapter 11

Dance Prep

There was always a lot of work in preparing for any one of the dances... wood to be cut for the fires, stones to be gathered for the sweat lodges, and if not already built, the building of the sheltered dance circles called *arbors*, the structure of the sweat lodge itself, the organizing and gathering of food for the kitchen, the maintenance and care of the grounds, the care and keeping of the drums, coordination of transportation and accommodation where necessary, and so on.

And to this day it never ceases to amaze me that so many people would come at their own expense from many different parts of the world to dance or *serve as volunteers* on the support crew.

Who knows what it is within us that calls or pulls us onto a spiritual path as this? Some might say it is God. Others might say it is a person's destiny. Yet others might say it is simply urgings of the heart. Maybe it doesn't make any difference other than to recognize that "you showed up and said yes"... yes to chopping wood, carrying water, whatever might be needed to serve *the people*, in this case, the dance and the dancers.

Though similarities to Native American culture are evident in this dance, the African, Mayan and other influences are just as evident. From the vision I received in 1996, a new form had emerged... a *global singing dance* that, we've been told by Jewish Rabbis and South African Sangomas, is a fulfilling of prophecy.

Whether this is true or not, I don't know. I only know that something had been born here that seemed to be answering a need in these chaotic times.

Chapter 12

Changes

It was in early spring with trees, flowers and all the woodland creatures bustling with new life, that the *youth dance* was to again take place. This time on Jonas and Sarah's land.
As we had done a number of dances on this land, all was done with great respect and joy, and we anticipated the same or better for this particular *youth dance.*

The week the dance was to begin, John and I had dinner with Jonas & Sarah. It was here, for the first time in all the years we had known Jonas, that we learned of his concerns as to our use of water in our dances, particularly that we have a bowl of water standing in the direction of the East Gate. You see, Jonas had been taught in a particular Native American tradition for more than fifteen years. And in his words, the forms he was taught have been around for thousands of years. He was having a challenge with our having both water and fire in the East gate, which is contrary to his teachings around his people's ceremonial dance. This may seem inconsequential to some, but for someone steeped in a particular tradition it could present challenges; much like asking someone of the Jewish faith to use the Christian symbol of the cross rather than the Jewish star to acknowledge a certain aspect of their beliefs. This isn't about what is right or wrong. It is about what is different.

As I write this, a quote from Rumi comes to mind. "Out beyond ideas of right doing and wrong doing, there is a field. I'll meet you there." At the time, it seemed we four were doing our best to find that field.

Jonas, Sarah and we talked for some time, our words often filled with emotion. John and I appreciated Jonas's concern. At the same time, we tried to help him see that *this* dance for which I had been given a clear vision was a different dance from the one of his teachings and tradition, and therefore its form and purpose were different.

Finally, we came up with a compromise each of us was willing to live with. The water in the East, which I was shown in my vision, would remain. We would add another bowl of water in the West to honor Jonas's tradition.

It was then that Jonas shared his concern that something on his land was "out of balance." Though he didn't say this directly, John and I both read this to mean that he thought it was the two of us who were bringing imbalance onto his land. Perhaps he meant others as well but the impact was singularly focused in those moments. We were stunned. I wanted to shout, "Don't you see? This *is* what this dance does! It brings balance. But first, it brings to light anything in the people and/or the land that needs to be looked at and dealt with so that balance *can* take place!" This could mean occurrences in the past generations as well as the present, all of which in some way were still in the land.

But I didn't say any of these things. I was in a strange kind of paralysis. I found myself silently praying, "God, what do you want me to do?" I didn't want to get *stuck in form* but I also wanted to stay in integrity with the vision I had been given. Feeling vulnerable and in shock, I asked for clarity and courage.

I reflect back on this moment and realize that had I known then what I know now, I may have cancelled the dance… or at least moved it to a different location. But through the eyes of friendship, I trusted. And with John's support and help, we moved forward.

Chapter 13

Angel

Just before the dance began, I was sitting by the sweatlodge fire. A beautiful little five-year old girl, with deep dark eyes, quietly crawled into my lap. At first she said nothing. She just kept looking at me. Then, in a clear child's voice, she said, "I love you." I felt the swell of tears and took a slow deep breath. Somehow, without knowing why, in that moment I knew this particular *youth dance* was important and for reasons I couldn't see at the time. My job was to be as clear as possible and let love guide me. After all, this was a dance for the children, for our own future and future generations.

We had a strong crew. And as most crew members had helped many times before in other dances on this land, John and I trusted them to know their jobs. Therefore, neither of us took time in the pre-dance crew meeting to address the uniqueness of a *youth dance* and the effect it might have on the crew. This was something we both soon regretted.

Indeed, this particular crew was highly competent and completely dedicated. Our assumption came in believing their veteran experience of skills inside a ceremonial dance would serve them adequately in a *youth dance.* For some this was certainly true. For others, however, this truth took a different twist.

The time came for the dance to start. With each dancer in his or her place in the dance arbor, with each crew member in place, serving as a drummer, a water/fire keeper, a kitchen angel, a server within or without the arbor… no matter what the role, the drum sounded a single beat. Dancers stood and the first sounds and movement began. The *youth dance* was now officially underway.

Soon into the dance I became aware that something had gone "wonky" (as our British friends might say) with the energy of the crew. It was then that I remembered, with painful awareness, that it is, indeed, inside these particular dances that "stuff" in one's own childhood that may never have been dealt with, would very likely find its way to the surface to be processed, manifesting itself through emotions and fear.

Later, I also saw how much a collective imagination would play a part in helping to goad the aftermath situation that developed one week later.

Chapter 14

Rain

In the initial part of the dance, John and I were to lead the dancers around the outside of the arbor, honoring, with song, all directions and the ancestors who had brought us there. I remember, at one point, seeing Jonas (who rarely came to the dances). Suddenly, without warning, I found myself distracted. My focus was no longer on the dancers but was on Jonas, the conversation we'd had earlier in the week, and the changes we had made around the water.

For a brief moment, I struggled internally with a sense of inadequacy and then heard the words of Sai Baba, "keep your eyes on me." It took a few minutes to find my center again. This small incident also helped to keep me centered throughout the dance. At no time from that moment on, was there any question of my total focus and energy being with the dancers, as well as the crew, and the welfare of all. As a dance Chief and particularly as the visionary for the dance itself, this was my sacred responsibility.

Shortly after the dance began, it started to rain. We've a Native friend who calls water, including rain, "liquid light." It rained most of the weekend, blessing us. At the same time, the rain was causing logistical challenges... MUD… lots of it! I remember Sarah, who was on the water/fire team, saying at the onset of the rain, "Let it come!" And it did. I've often wondered, in retrospect, if she remembered what she had said.

Through it all, the dancers were amazing. These young people, who had survived ungodly abuses in one form or another for much of their lives, were the epitome of courage, as were the adults who danced with them. The rain, with the movement and sound, helped to pull from them much of what was needed to be released. It did the same for the crew.

Something else was also happening. I began to notice a reluctance, even a confusion, on the part of our water/fire team to care for the water and fire in a way that was needed. Particularly, this was true around the water.

When I was given the vision of the dance, I was shown how the *water* and *fire* would work together to create a birthing canal for the old to be released and the new to be born. The water in this dance is very similar to an embryonic fluid. It nourishes the dancers while at the same time, helps to carry away that which no longer serves them. The fire is the vehicle through which the old is then released and the new life emerges.

This is all metaphoric, of course. What is actually happening with the dancer is that each person is fasting and singing sounds (no words) created in the moment while moving in his or her path within the arbor. The experience is to move one beyond thought and into a deeper heartspace. Here each person is given the space and opportunity to let go of anger, rage, pain, any experience that has created limitation for this individual, so that he or she no longer has to carry this around for the rest of his/her life. We call this "clearing the hollow bone." Surrounded by love and an experienced crew, a person can then reenter life much like a newborn.

Because the *waterkeeper's* job is to honor the water throughout the dance, she or he may work with the water in a caring way, much as a *firekeeper* works with the fire. This may be singing, stirring, whatever the waterkeeper is guided to do, as long as it is done with respect and loving intent. More and more, as this dance has evolved, the same person(s) who is caring for the fire also now cares for the water as well, one being a different aspect of the whole.

As the *youth dance* progressed, the rain increased and it became apparent that those on the water/fire team were in conflict with their roles. Each member of the two men/ two women team represented a different tradition. I saw very soon that three of the team were getting *stuck in form*, rather than allowing themselves to be in the energy and new teachings being given them through this particular dance. Each wanted to do it a different way. Yet, because I never doubted their intent and their hearts, I trusted the dance would carry them, indeed, would teach them.

One with imagination might ask, "Was there so much drama around the water, including the rain, because something had been compromised in the beginning by putting a bowl of water in the West, thus changing the energy flow of the dance?" The skeptic would say, "I doubt it." Whatever the truth, the water was doing its work. It was bringing people's fears and wounds in the land to the surface to be dealt with. This became overwhelmingly evident one week later.

Part IV

BETRAYAL

"Maybe it isn't about the dance at all,
but how we treat each other
as we create the experience."

—Jeanne White Eagle
(from a dream)

Chapter 15

Face of Fear

During the week that followed the *youth dance*, I became sick with a bronchial infection. Even before the dance, my immune system was low. I had made plans to visit my daughter in Washington State in a few days, but wanted first to give my body time to recuperate.

The next weekend after the *youth dance,* John was to lead a different kind of dance, also a dance for the people and one whose unique energy calls in the Star Beings. Again, this one was to be held on Jonas and Sarah's land. I was not to participate in this dance as I was quite weak from the bronchitis. And I had had enough experiences in my life with bronchial pneumonia to know that I didn't want to chance getting it again.

As always when we were in that part of the world, John and I were blessed to be staying in the home of an old and dear friend, Lonie, who endeared herself to us through her deep love and respect for nature and all the forest creatures, including raccoons, deer and an inordinate number of stray cats who seemed to easily find their way to her door. We often said there was a sign in the woods that plainly read in animal talk: "Eat at Lonie's place."

Friday

And so, on Friday morning John set out for the danceground while, in our dear friend's home, I stayed still and in a healing space, anticipating the visit to my daughter.

Shortly after leaving, John phoned to say that his dance had been cancelled. I listened in a frozen stillness as he shared that the danceground was a pool of mud, created from the prior weekend at the *youth dance*. Also, there was a strange odor emitting from the North side of the arbor. He asked if I would come and participate in a meeting with the people. I sank inside. I was very ill, running a fever and had no energy to do this. But not wanting him to be without support, I came.

Before leaving for the meeting, I called a close friend of ours in Vermont, who is a world-class seer. For the reader who doesn't get into this kind of thing, it might help to know that our friend speaks six languages, can read a thousand pages in one day, and has often served as a consultant for such global corporations as IBM and Hewlett Packard. In a word, our friend is well-grounded. Fascinating person! And brilliant!

The information she gave was interesting. She said that much had happened on the land where Jonas and Sarah now lived, including the killing of black slaves in the 1800s that were put into a mass grave. Apparently too, there had been a chemical drainoff from an industrial activity on a nearby mountain in the 1930s that found its way into the soil and was now surfacing. The last piece was that there was livestock sewage seepage surfacing in the soil as well. All of this working together was what was helping to produce the odors emitting from the ground.

With so much rain the week before and the churning of the soil from the feet of the dancers in the *youth dance* who themselves were processing through their own quagmires, it was little wonder that the ground had responded in the way it had. The result was the land was now tired and needed to rest. This was the belief of Jonas and Sarah. John and I were more than willing to support them in this.

To have allowed ourselves to step back and breathe, making a conscious choice to simply move on from that point with patience, insight and blessings for the land and all who had come to dance, would have been the wisest path to take at that time. Rather, this is what happened…

Fear reared its head and the mass consciousness of the group responded… with trepidation, apprehension, and suspicion.

Saturday Morning

Several people had traveled long distances to participate in John's dance. Now that it was cancelled, John didn't want to simply send the people back to their homes. Instead, it was decided that on Saturday after Friday's meeting where the causes and fate of the weekend's dance were discussed, a further meeting would be spent in group dialogue.

The morning session of that Saturday was a good one. People had slept overnight and had been given time to reflect on information coming from Friday's meeting, sharing ideas and possibilities. Had the time together been concluded at that point, most likely all would have ended congenially, given the circumstances.

I, in the meantime, was struggling physically, doing my own dance with bronchitis. I committed to staying, however, to support John. As a result, my life changed forever.

Chapter 16

Saturday Afternoon

The second half of Saturday's meeting began benignly enough. Though had I been more astute, I would have paid more attention to the energy shift in some of the people. The truth is, I don't remember who said what first. I do remember that what happened was a one-hundred eighty degree turn in group dynamics from our time together in the morning.

Without warning, I was being attacked. It was subtle at first and came with gentle stealth that blindsided both John and me.

Rather than speaking of John's dance, as was anticipated, several in the group (thirty five to forty persons present) wanted to talk about what challenged them in the *youth dance* the week before. This must have been somewhat puzzling to the people who were not present for that dance.

The following comments are examples of what started to surface. "I saw demonic faces in the water." "Why do you stir the water? It feels evil somehow." Regarding the fire, "that is not how I was taught." Regarding the tree that stands in the center of the arbor, "I was taught that the energy of the pole moves in a different direction." Regarding the request to offer thanks to the crew, "we shouldn't have to say thank you for the work we do. That is a given." "I saw you split into two people." "Who was that large being standing behind you?" On and on went the comments, each coming with such a force that one by one they were like sharp daggers being thrust into my body.

It wasn't so much the comments themselves as it was the energy that was gathering in the group. With each question and comment building on itself, the energy was slowly turning chaotic and bordered on abuse and a strange kind of "mass hysteria." I'm not sure the group was even aware of what was actually happening. Certainly some individuals were, but the collective was stronger and its path was already set in motion.

I struggled to stay centered. I listened as best I could. It was important to me to hear each person, hoping that each one also felt heard. This is what John and I encourage in the conflict resolution work we do. And in my heart and mind, it was crucial that "I walk my talk," especially with this community whom we had come to love over the years.

There were legitimate and clear answers for each question and comment directed toward me, but I was so shocked and weak that I simply sat and answered only what came to me in the moment. All the while, I was silently praying, "God, please help me come from love." Over and over and over I was saying this internally, as it gave me some stability in the storm that had begun. I also found myself doing something I learned when I had a dangerous bout of pancreatitis some years ago. That with every inhale, I would silently breathe in the word *Love.* With every exhale, I would breathe out the word *Love.* I would do this until it became a gentle mantra that would help me through the pain. Once again, I found myself creating this mantra, as I listened to the people that Saturday.

Some of the answers I might have given were simply these: " If one is seeing demonic faces in the water, it was likely a reflection of something within that person asking for healing;" "If the water was being stirred it was to create the same circumstance that occurs when the embryonic fluids are moving to clear, purify and nurture the new life being born;" "The energy of the center tree or pole, in this particular dance, happens in a way to best serve the dancer. It, in effect, is the umbilical cord that brings nourishment from the Source into the new life;" "As to the fire, in this dance, it works in tandem with the water and is to be treated with great respect." (Here I remember the beautiful teachings given to me while living briefly with the Mayan Elders in Central America.) "To say *'Thank you'* is one of the highest ways of showing respect as we each are a reflection of Great Spirit. It used to be that the way of prayer for the Cherokee was always and only prayers of gratitude;" "The being you saw over me was an angel feeding me light." The teachings are many. But perhaps one of the greatest is one taught to me first by my father, and later reinforced by two other dear and wise elders, Willis Harman and Joseph Rael, *"Don't get stuck in form."*

This wisdom was in me to give to the group, but in those moments the words wouldn't come. So I listened. Comment after comment came, followed by questions, most colored with judgment and criticism. And though I was willing to do what I could to answer them, I was more perplexed with the energy of the group. They had turned into something that might be compared to the energy of the Spanish Inquisition. At least, this is how it felt to me. I was the target.

It is important to say that I never doubted the sincerity of the hearts of the individuals, but I did become overwhelmingly sad when I realized as a collective they didn't seem to see what was actually happening. Sarah told me months after, "There was no doubt. It was a witch-hunt." My question was why? These were people we have loved and trusted, some for many years. They, in turn, have loved and cared for us. How was it possible that they en masse would turn on me like a pack of hungry dogs?

Granted, there were some individuals in the group who spoke out and did what they could to shift the energy. I will be forever grateful to them. But the three people who could have stopped it all, Jonas, Sarah and John, basically said nothing. John might have spoken up more strongly than he did but I believe he felt he was also being attacked through the assault I was experiencing, and was perhaps in as much shock as I was. Sarah, at one point, ran out of the room. For whatever reason she did this, my experience was one of abandonment. Jonas sat with eyes closed and head bent, saying nothing.

Except for the handful of souls who were willing to speak their truths, I felt completely abandoned and alone. My body began to respond with involuntary uncontrollable shaking. One of the women across the room saw this. She came quickly to wrap a blanket around me, bending over to hold me as my body broke down.

It was a strange sensation, this. I felt helpless and naked while in a kind of objective confusion as those on either side of me did nothing. On one side was my beloved husband who, as I've said, was in his own state of paralysis and shock. While on the other side was a very dear and old friend who herself was a revered Native medicine woman. It was as though a scene out of a fantasy movie of black magic was being enacted where a dark spell was being cast over the people.

Part of me kept asking, "What have I done that would bring such an attack?" Because of my own conditioning as a facilitator in conflict resolution, I couldn't bring myself to leave the group at that point, knowing the primary way through chaos is to *move through it*, not ignore or avoid it.

I also couldn't step into the role of facilitating the conflict, as I was the target. I loved these people, and whatever they chose to do to or with me, I was clear I needed to keep coming from love and truth as best I could. I did feel anger at one point and voiced this to the group, not by accusing them but by owning my own feelings and thoughts around what was happening. This was short lived, however. I quickly sank back into a place of incredulity, not wanting to believe that what was happening was actually occurring.

Reflecting some time later on the whole situation, I realized I had gotten a glimpse of occurrences throughout human history in which a person has been either ostracized from a community (as was made evident in Nathaniel Hawthorne's *The Scarlet Letter*), or was killed in some gruesome fashion as retribution for whatever accusation had been thrust upon the unfortunate soul. The time of the Spanish Inquisition is such an example. Men and especially women were falsely accused of committing crimes against the faith of the Catholic Church and were subsequently burned at the stake or tortured and then killed in whatever manner and way the Church saw fit. There is little doubt as to what my own fate would have been had I lived during these times.

The moment at which I thought my heart would break was when one dear friend, who had come to me years ago with great love and honor saying, "You don't ever need to worry. I will always have your back," questioned me in such a way that I felt as though we were inside circumstances more fit for medieval times than for the 21st century.

What did stun me was that no one, not one person, asked about the welfare of the dancers themselves, those who had actually danced the *youth dance.* No one asked how *they, the dancers* were doing, what had been their experience. It could have been because none of the dancers were present. However, the omission of any concern was interesting. I said this to the group. Having already received follow-up reports from some of the youth and parents through the week, all were doing great. They had felt loved, safe and deeply cared for in the dance, and were already asking when the next one would happen. But the group at the Saturday meeting could not hear this. They had moved into chaos and inside the state of chaos, it is almost impossible to "hear" what is being said. Chaos produces an energy that fosters confusion, finger pointing, frenetic rhythm and heated interaction.

Yet even in the chaos, it amazed me that no one seemed to show much interest in the dancers. Always in the dances, the dancer comes first, because they dance for us all. And something must have happened in a good way at the dance or the result of the dancers' experience would not have been as powerful as it was.

The group instead, was hung up on the "form" of the dance itself. The only rational answer I could find was that those on the crew who were caught in *form* and who ultimately experienced fear, confusion, apparitions, hallucinations and the like, were perhaps the very ones whose own "stuff" was getting triggered. Perhaps they were being given an opportunity to look closely at and deal with their own fears, "stuckness," and/or belief systems.

Something shared with me months after that weekend meeting was a conversation that had taken place *prior to the youth dance* by a few of the crew who, sitting around over a cup of coffee, were talking about witches and beliefs coming down from the Middle Ages. Though this conversation may have been harmless at the time, it may also have helped to set the stage for what occurred in both the dance and the meeting the following week.

As for the meeting itself, it lasted, it seemed, for an eternity. Finally, when my physical body was near to collapse, I stood up, told the people I loved them but that it was time now for me to go.

Several people, some of whom had spoken out against what they saw happening, came up to hug me. When I got to the car, I cried, uncontrollably. I didn't really know what had happened. I was still in shock. All I knew was that something extraordinary had just occurred. And the sense of having been completely abandoned by those in whom I had placed such trust, now was absolute.

I understood better then *how* Bosnia happened. Utter Betrayal.

Part V

CRUCIBLE

"I hope God will give me the courage and the sense to forgive them. I have no anger against them. I am only sorry for their ignorance and their narrowness. I know that they sincerely believe that what they are doing today is right and proper. I have no reason, therefore, to be angry with them."

— Mahatma Gandhi
(following a brutal beating in
Natal, South Africa, 1896)

Chapter 17

Flight

The days, weeks, and months that followed that fateful meeting were filled with a myriad of experiences that collectively would have been fodder for Dante's Inferno. In fact, Dante in his "Nine Levels of Hell" even speaks of the lowest and most severe level of hell as being the Betrayal of Trust.
For John and me, the bottom had dropped out. The foundational trust we had had so unconditionally in those we had called dear friends, was gone. Betrayal and loss took on a whole new dimension for each of us.

The meeting had taken place on a Saturday. That night and on through Sunday, concerned individuals (including Sarah) were calling to check on me. I told John that I wanted to speak with no one. I couldn't. I was numb from all that had taken place. I needed complete solitude in those first hours.

Strangely, I wasn't angry. I was still in a state of shock… and very clear that whatever happened, I must will myself to deal with the whole situation, as much as was possible, from a place of love. Now, this may sound silly, even unrealistic to some. But to me it was important, albeit an uninvited, even crucial, test. Given that I had made a personal commitment many years ago, to do what good I could to make a positive difference in the world, if I didn't handle what had just happened to me in a good and honorable way, then everything I had given myself to would have been for nothing.

I kept remembering something Chief Joseph of the Nez Perce Indians said when, in the 1800s, he and his tribe were captured by the U.S. Cavalry a few miles from the Canadian border. When his warriors were urging him to fight, he laid down his weapons and said,

"...I will fight no more forever."

Though I wasn't due to fly to Seattle to my daughter, Jenny, for another week, I made the decision on Sunday after the Saturday meeting to not wait. I left early Monday morning.

At Jenny's, I found myself able to get distance from the weekend's trauma. There was safety and solace in being over two thousand miles away and being in the company of my daughter. In rare moments I found myself grinning at years gone by, early on in the lives of both my beloved children, John T and Jenny, when the three of us would bond together as a single parent family, supporting and loving each other through life's dramas and daily challenges. Here again, I came into that safe haven. This time, my child had become a dear and much needed friend.

The two weeks at Jenny's gave me time to get perspective, so that when I returned to my husband, John, I was in a better place than when I had left.

Chapter 18

Dream

The first month was filled with endless tears and great sadness. My waking hours, it seemed, were a constant prayer… "Spirit, help me deal with the whole situation in a good way." I kept asking, "Jesus, what would you do? Sai Baba, what would you do? Gandhi, what would you do?"

I prayed for a sign, something that I couldn't miss. For those first few weeks, I simply kept getting "Be still. Be patient." A lot easier said than done! But because I was determined to find a loving way through it all, I managed to wait… wait until an answer came. And it did. Through a dream.

I dreamed John and I gave a party. The guests were those who had participated in that Saturday meeting at Jonas and Sarah's. At the party, John and I did a large Give-Away, a ceremony to gift to our friends items that have personal worth and value to the two of us. It was a joyous occasion.

When I woke from the dream, I said to John, "We're going to throw a party and we're going to do a Give-Away." John's forehead crinkled a bit and then there came a breath of resignation. At first, he didn't seem to be particularly excited about the idea, but warmed up to it when I shared an understanding that had come to me over time and was reminded of in the dream.

Having worked with both abused children and abused spouses as well as those of varying ages and cultures who have survived warring conflict, I'm very aware that the impetus of responsibility for the hurt inflicted, falls on the aggressor, the one or ones carrying out the abuse. Yet, *after* the act, when all is said and done, the one who has the *power* to initiate and bring about true healing for both parties involved is *the one who has been abused.*

This is not to say sincere apologies from the aggressor are not important, indeed critical. It is to say that the healing at a cellular level may require more than an apology can bear. This is assuming the one who has brought abuse has the strength of character and heart to offer an apology where one is due. Oddly, and this certainly happened in the Saturday meeting, many of those who joined in the collective abuse may not have even been consciously aware of what they had done until some time later, if at all.

Because we had become close friends with so many of Jonas and Sarah's community over a number of years, I realize that it was possible that some who had participated in the verbal and energetic chaos of the meeting that one weekend, once they recognized what had happened, might themselves not know how to respond, interact and enter back into relationship with John and me. It was clear that some were embarrassed, while others were simply at a loss as to what to do to heal what had happened.

Here is where my dream provided insight and an answer. John and I would take the initiative. We would throw a party. We would invite the community and see who turned up.

Chapter 19

Divine Hand

I have to admit I was a little nervous. I wasn't crazy about putting myself in the line of fire, only to be shot down again. Yet, I knew that if I was ever going to get beyond what had happened that Saturday weeks ago, I needed to let go and trust there was a Divine hand in this somewhere.

I kept thinking of that biblical story of Daniel and the lions' den. When Daniel entered the den of lions, an angel showed up. I guess I was hoping that an angel would show up at our party.

And so, we put the invitation out there, naming a date and the location. The party would take place at the home of our dear friend, Lonie.

To prepare for the Giveaway we wanted to do at the party, we went through our belongings. Because of our choice of lifestyle we didn't have all that much materially. This was a conscious choice the two of us made in the mid-90s when we left the corporate world to begin the peace work we now do. What we did have in material possessions were mostly the bare necessities and a few items, precious gifts given to us by friends from around the world. It was from this treasured collection of abundance that we chose what to put onto the Giveaway blanket.

The day of the party was filled with reflection and prayer. I wanted to be clear and centered within myself so that when I looked into the eyes of whoever came, I could do so with integrity and with kindness.

Still, I was a bit nervous. I wasn't sure what to expect. Though I could make an intuitive guess, I actually was not able to predict how the evening might go. I did know, however, that I was totally in charge of me, of my own actions and reactions. I was responsible for my own behavior no matter what might transpire.

Nelson Mandela has long been one of my heroes. When I think back to the night of the party, I remember the poem "Invictus" by William Ernest Henley that so inspired Mandela and gave him strength go on when it seemed life had turned against him:

Invictus

Out of the night that covers me,
Black as the Pit from pole to pole,
I thank whatever gods may be
For my unconquerable soul.

In the fell clutch of circumstance
I have not winced nor cried aloud.
Under the bludgeonings of chance
My head is bloody, but unbowed.

Beyond this place of wrath and tears
Looms but the Horror of the shade,
And yet the menace of the years
Finds, and shall find, me unafraid.

It matters not how strait the gate,
How charged with punishments the scroll.

I am the master of my fate:
I am the captain of my soul.

The other thought is a direct quote of Mandela, *"Forgiveness liberates the soul. It removes fear."* It was from this kind of conviction and inspiration that I found the courage to trust in the choice I had made to follow the wisdom of my dream.

To both John's and my surprise, except for a few who had traveled long distances to participate in the recent dances and a couple of others in the community with prior commitments, everyone else showed up at the party. After some tentative "hellos," it turned out to be a fun evening, hopefully for all there.

When we did the Giveaway, I remember looking into the individual faces and thinking of how much I loved each person there. While we were all gathered around the Giveaway blanket, in a somewhat shaky voice I shared, "Whatever else you do, remember to care for each other, honor each other's differences. Love each other." Nothing else was said.

I do remember how fragile John and I both were in those moments, each of us doing our best to trust that we were doing the right thing.

Chapter 20

Saibaba

Within a week, after the party, we left to go overseas. We were to be gone for several weeks, returning only for a few days, before leaving again for seven months. With so much distance, and eventually time, between us and the States, I was aware that even though the healing had begun, something was still lingering. I could feel it in my gut. It gnawed away, subtly, silently for weeks… weeks that became months. What was it? I couldn't put my finger on it. I just knew something was incomplete, still undone, unfinished.

My body, which had been fragile for all those days during and since the incident at Jonas and Sarah's, was showing signs of serious injury in my back and hips. I was finding it harder and harder to walk. Healers and doctors showed up from everywhere, each with his or her own prognosis. In Croatia, Bosnia, Israel, Germany, Ireland, Norway and finally South Africa, I was treated with loving hands and brilliant insight.

Some were saying that what was happening to me was a remnant of the pancreatitis attack I had had a few years back. Others said I was developing a scoliosis, that my spinal column was deteriorating in places, etc. etc. Some of what was said was, indeed, confirmed by X-rays.

After several months, I was guided to a doctor from India, living and operating a practice in a small village in South Africa. When I first saw him I got the immediate impression that I was looking into the eyes of Sai Baba, one of India's most beloved Avatars. So gentle. So kind and wise.

John and I were invited to have a seat in his small office. His first comment was a question directed at me, "Can you think of something, perhaps an emotional event that might have occurred at some point in the last months that would lead to the condition you're in now?" I looked straight into his eyes and answered "Yes, there is an incident that happened many months ago.."

Without my having to say any more than that, he replied with a knowing smile, "Exactly!" Then he went on to say, simply and almost matter-of-factly, "You will heal yourself."

John, who was seated next to me, grinned and said, "Now you're speaking our language."

This gentle doctor had been right. Within four weeks my physical body had completely healed. My emotional body, however, had a few more hurdles to go.

Chapter 21

Anger?

It was at some point during the Christmas holidays that a flash of insight came. John and I were in Croatia at the time. We were spending the holidays with dear friends on the Isle of Krk in a small village called Malinska. I remember waking up in the early morning, sitting straight up in the bed and saying, "I know what it is that keeps hanging on! I'm angry! I'm angry with Jonas!! I'm angry that he didn't see that he was asking me to change the sacred vision I was given to fit his perception of how he thought it ought to be. I'm angry that he said he had to come along after us (and others) and 'clean up.' I'm angry that [on that painful Saturday], he said nothing. Nothing!" The words fell out, one on top of the other, like a rushing torrent. I spewed them out as though they were hot lava pouring from some kind of an emotional volcano, while John listened patiently. Tears followed. After it was done and everything was out, John and I were able then to talk about it more rationally. I felt relief. Finally, after all these months I was at last able *to identify*, admit and say out loud what I had been feeling. This was the unfinished piece. It was done. This excruciating journey, maybe now, was over. At least it seemed that way in those moments.

It didn't take long for me to see that underneath the anger was a deep hurt. A deep *sadness.* Though we had had our differences over time, I had come to love and respect Jonas as a brother and a friend. In the beginning there had been a mutual sharing of wisdoms and teachings. There had been a mutual respect for each other's ways. But over time this changed. I watched him become more steeped in a certain Native tradition and from John's and my perception, "stuck in form." On one hand I respected Jonas's absolute dedication to this path. On the other hand I became saddened that this brother of mine, whom I had come to love as a dear friend, in our eyes, seemed not to see what was happening. There seemed to be little room for flexibility, change, and finally, evolvement.

Of course, looking through his eyes he might have felt something similar about us, particularly me. I don't know.

Neither John nor I had spent so many years learning one particular tradition. Rather we have been exposed to and learned from Masters over a period of time of many traditions, coming to a conclusion that the underlying premise of most is one of reverence for life and ultimately love for all. And it doesn't take a genius to know that all traditions have their fanatics, those that have little to no tolerance for anything but the power pieces of a belief system, indeed negating entirely the very heart of a tradition which is not the form itself but is the purpose for which the form came about in the first place.

I not once saw Jonas as a fanatic. Rather I saw him as a soul searching for a truth within which he could feel safe. Perhaps at some level, each of us does this, whether we do so consciously or unconsciously. I also experienced Jonas as someone who had within himself an innate wisdom that he was very capable of sharing much of the time but that was often shadowed by some deep personal demons that he may not have even been aware of.

Whatever was going on with Jonas, whatever my perceptions, accurate or not, I knew I had to keep "clearing my own hollow bone," or as the ancient biblical writings said "taking the mote out of my own eye." I had to recognize and deal with any anger or other unresolved feelings within myself before I could find peace. And in this, it was my job to do the best I could to be in integrity with myself at all times. Anyone else's perception of me, including Jonas's, was filtered through and measured in accordance with that person's willingness to clear himself or herself of anything, emotions, memories, etc. that clog up the spiritual mechanism of who he or she is as a sacred being. That was their responsibility. Not mine. I had enough to do in keeping myself in check.

Chapter 22

Stuck in Form

"Stuck in form." What does it mean? Though I had lived with this concept much of my life, I still asked this question because I wanted to be certain, as much as was possible, that neither John nor I were getting caught in this elusive web. It was in a dream that insight came around the whole concept of "form."
Forms, no matter what they are, be they ceremonial, religious, scientific, traditional, etc., are like props used in a play or movie. Stage or movie props help to give order and support so that those watching the movie might perceive the message of the script better. But just as movie props are not the goal of a movie, *forms* within themselves are not the goal of a *purpose.* They are a vehicle through which a message might more clearly be conveyed.

And when it is necessary, *the form changes* to better support the evolution of the perceptual reality of that time. Again, a movie analysis can be used. How many movies are there *remakes* of, to better "fit the times?"

Another analogy might be a *glass* holding water. The glass itself is important in the sense that it allows a drink to be taken without the water dispersing in different directions, getting everything wet except the inside of our bodies. But, if one is wanting a drink, the goal, then, is not the glass. The *goal* is to quench our thirst. Therefore, the glass is a *form* that serves as a container for the water. Yet it is not the only form of container that can carry water. Indeed, there are containers for water of all different sizes, kinds and colors. They may take the shape of jugs, cups, pitchers, tanks, etc. It then becomes the choice of the user as to what container meets the need at that moment in time. Whichever choice is made, the purpose of satisfying one's thirst will be met. One might say the *goal* of a religion is to quench the thirst of the soul in its journey to remember its spiritual origin. And is it not true that in the arena of religion there are many different forms (rituals, disciplines, belief structures, etc.), and in the end all religions are pointing to the same conclusion, that of recognizing and honoring a higher and divine Consciousness, whether within or outside of ourselves?

Where we, as a species, get into trouble is when we insist there is only *one* way to do a thing or that we do something because "this is the way it has been done for thousands of years." It reminds me of the story of a young woman learning to cook a ham, who saws off the end of it as directed by her mother. She then asks, "Mother, why do we always saw off the end of the ham before we cook it?" Her mother replies, "Because that is the way your grandmother always did it." So they go to the grandmother and ask the same question. Her answer is simple. "Because that is the way your great grandmother always did it." As the great grandmother was still living, they all go to her and ask why it was that she always cut off the end of the ham before cooking it. She smiles and says, "Because I didn't have a pan large enough to hold the whole ham." So when someone says to me, "I do it this way because this is the way it has been done for thousands of years," I find myself stepping back to get perspective.

Chapter 23

Waking Up

Once I had come to grips with the piece I had been searching for, i.e., the recognition of anger, more to the point, a *sadness* I was feeling but hadn't been able to access, I really thought this might be all that was needed to complete this strange odyssey I had been on. And then, it was only a day or two after that I had another dream.

The message was revealing and powerful. It was a simple statement…

"Maybe it isn't about the dance at all,
but how we treat each other as we create the experience."

Suddenly, it was clear. Whatever the path, whatever the form someone has chosen, it is important to ask these questions… how are we treating each other as we interact in our daily dramas and conditions, particularly when under stress of time, circumstance or dogma? Are we being kind? Are we being patient? This is the teaching that the masters like Jesus, Buddha, and all others were saying to us in their own way,

"Love one another."

Here was the pivotal message, overriding everything else! Why had it taken me so long to see this clearly? Certainly I had been raised with this message throughout childhood, and had done the best I could to live this in every aspect of my life. But now something was different. I experienced a level of understanding that I hadn't had before. Something went "kerchunk" and fell into place deep within me. It was so simple. So clear. I found myself in a state of awareness that allowed me to touch the deepest meaning of what I would call a *divine truth*... simply, *Love one another.*

If it is true that Love is all there is, which has been espoused by poets, philosophers and sages for eons, then anything else is *illusion* and therefore, doesn't even exist, not in the way we think it does. This means our dramas, our forms, all that we perceive is transitory. And how we remember this is by the simple act of reaching out to the *other*... by *loving one another.*

Having awakened to this deeper reality, the question then became, "Would I have the wisdom and strength to apply what was showing itself to me, to the issue at hand... the unresolved sadness wedged inside the crevices of my soul?"

Chapter 24

Challenged

The crux of the matter was this. Jonas mattered. Sarah mattered. And in the moment when it was most needed, I felt our bond of friendship was breaking. How could this have happened? Always we were able to work through our differences with care and love. I never doubted Jonas's heart and certainly honored his right to move on the path he was now choosing. After all these years, if he was choosing a path so different that it wouldn't allow the sacred dance I was given in vision to occur on his land, that was his prerogative as the land's caretaker.

It was simply that now John and I both felt our integrity was being challenged… our intention. This was hard to swallow when John and I both had tried to come from a good place at all times, honoring and loving the land and the people who had brought us into this circle years before.

When I think back on it, there is not one time that John or I stepped onto Jonas's land without great respect. As an example, before each dance was to occur, I would come onto the danceground in the wee hours of the morning prior to the first day of the dance, before the sun came up and before anyone else awoke. Here I would offer prayers and simple ceremony asking *permission* of the ancestors, the land and all life on her to bring the dance there. At the same time I was clear that it was the land that had called *us*. The invitation had come from the land, from the ancestors, from Jonas and Sarah. We had responded by showing up and saying "yes." To do the ceremony asking *permission* was a way of giving respect. To do the ceremony to honor the *invitation* was to give blessings of gratitude for this and for all the miracles that would happen. And always the closing prayer was, "Let only Love happen here." Each prayer, each song, each step taken, happened in a good way.

Though I myself was not raised on a reservation, I believe there must be something in my own Cherokee lineage that gets triggered, memories perhaps, that easily come forth when conditions call for it. Maybe it is a kind of instinct. I don't know. But since I was a child I knew the importance of caring for the land and those around me in a respectful way. And certainly part of this was a result of my own upbringing. But there was something deeper. There was a *knowing*. This became evident in later years, particularly when it came to doing things in a ceremonial way without ever having been shown the ceremonies themselves. This doesn't mean I haven't received guidance and teachings along the way. Indeed, I have. But the underlying understanding of the *why*, and most often the *how*, seemed to come instinctively. Some might say it was the spirits of those who have gone before that have guided me. Others might say it is genetic memory, perhaps even memory of past lives. Whatever the belief of the reader, what matters is that at no time did I (or John) come onto Jonas's land without full consciousness of the significance and magnitude of honoring Life and the land upon which Life's experiences took place.

For the most part, the gentle simple ceremonies that carried both John's and my prayers went unseen, before, during and after the dance. This way it allowed a humbler interaction with God, or Spirit. Because of this, I'm not aware that Jonas ever witnessed or even knew his land was being honored in such a loving way as it was. And it never dawned on me or John to tell Jonas what we were doing. That would have felt like something coming from the ego and that, in itself, would have been out of integrity.

I can honestly say that with every step and breath, we consciously were aware of the importance of caring for the land and the people. And so, one can appreciate the impact that John and I experienced when Jonas spoke of having to come along and "clean up after us."

In retrospect, perhaps this was Jonas's way of retracting the invitation he had given to us so many years before, to come to his land. An even more puzzling possibility.

Here was the clincher. With all that had happened, the night after the Saturday meeting, I came back in the early morning hours, shortly after midnight, and sang prayers of healing for the land, while at the same time asking forgiveness for anything I myself might have done unknowingly to bring separation into the community. No one saw. No one knew. It was simply the right and a good thing to do.

Chapter 25

More Dreams

When clarity came so profoundly to the surface of my consciousness that December morning in Croatia, I remembered yet another dream I had had that spring night following the conversation with Jonas where he shared that he was experiencing imbalance in the land. The dream was a simple one. *Jonas was sitting. I walked up, placed my hand on his heart and gently said, "This is what is out of balance."* In remembering this dream, was it possible that perhaps the "cleaning up" Jonas felt was needed, might have been what he needed to do with himself? If so, that was something for him to figure out. I was busy working on myself.

To identify anger and my deep sadness over Jonas's not saying anything in the Saturday meeting (in my presence), was monumental. I'm not even sure what he could have said had he spoken, but to remain so totally silent was devastating to me, particularly as it was he who had been so vocal in his concerns prior to the dances or the meeting. Granted, Sarah and John could have said or done something differently but in the days and weeks that followed, much was resolved in my heart where they were concerned. It was with Jonas, whom I had come to love as a brother, that I still felt something unfinished. *Recognizing* the anger and the *sadness* underneath was not enough. Something else was being asked of me. Alas! What?!

Chapter 26

Echoes

Going back over my journals, I've been interested to see the number of references to Jonas, Sarah and the Saturday incident which seemed to have taken place so long ago. It was clear that unresolved feelings were surfacing and crying out for resolve. It's as though for the better part of a year, a cloud of unrest hung over me. *Daily* I lived in a private hell of turmoil and unfinished "business." Here are just a few entries.

June 17, Germany: "I can't seem to get the community off my mind, particularly Jonas. There are some unresolved feelings inside me. I release it to you, God, to show me how to be with all this. Help me to "seek first the Kingdom of Heaven"… help what is out of balance to come back into balance… help us, dear God… show me the way."

July 9, Germany: "The whole situation that occurred at Jonas and Sarah's keeps creeping back into my consciousness. I pray for healing for me, for them, for the land and all. I still hurt. Please help, God."

July 13, Germany: "You know my heart, God, and I'm trusting healing at all levels can take place here. I ask for your guidance."

July 22, Croatia: Insight: Regarding the relationship with Jonas, Sarah and their community, "the way of Love is always the only way. All else is illusion."

August 11, USA: "…I woke up this morning with the image of Jesus shaking dust from his feet, a metaphor for our immediate journey with Jonas, Sarah and the community there at the moment. I'll keep holding them in my heart, surrounding them with Love."

August 12, USA: "…Regarding Jonas and Sarah, simply Love them. That opens the door for God to do the rest."

August 16, USA: "I realize how hurt and sad I continue to be. God, help me forgive.

August 19, USA: "Trust. Patience is my friend. Love is my guide."

August 21, USA: Insight: "When one is attached to the old ways then one cannot see the new clearly, as the strings of attachment 'clog the hollow bone.' Being in the Now is all we can experience when attachments are released… otherwise, there is struggle born in the soul that creates 'forgetting.'"

August 23, USA: "My heart is still heavy. Please help me, God."

August 26, USA: A moment of light: "Last night we laid aside two hours to give to the community before flying out for Ireland the next morning. This came about as a result of our having received several calls and emails from those in the community wanting to see us, before we left for what would be a seven month journey overseas. Here was the miracle. There was so much Love flowing that the whole anger issue didn't even arise. In fact, at one point, our dear friend, Ted, who over the months had given a sincere heartfelt apology for anything he might have said in that dance meeting that might have brought me pain, agreed with me that it isn't what we do but *how we are with each* *other* that is important. That night there was truly a healing happening within my own heart as well as John's and, I hope, for the others."

September 28, Norway: "I have done prayers for those who would hate me and I am remembering that forgiveness is so important, that my focus is to be on Love, trusting all else will fall into place. I will move forward as Love guides me."

September 30, Norway: "What I'm convinced of is that Jesus' teaching around "Love one another" is identical with what I'm being given, only in different words: '…Maybe it's about how we treat each other as we create the experience.'"

October 13, Norway: "My legs, especially my right hip, are causing me great challenge. I realize that somehow my pain may be unresolved feelings over what happened that Saturday."

October 21, Israel: "I realize that when I get into this place I find myself right now, that the only place left for me is SURRENDER."

November 22, South Africa: "I realized with a shock that this adventure with my back, which started after the dance meeting, is a direct result of the trust having been broken and my feeling as though I no longer have a home there [with Jonas and Sarah's community]."

December 9, South Africa: "My body truly is healing and is getting stronger. Yesterday was the first day I have walked without a limp in eight months. Yes!!"

December 21, Croatia: "Asking inside where home was, especially after the Saturday incident, this came, 'There is no need to worry where you will lay your head. Simply breathe and see the banquet that is laid out before you.'"

December 22, Croatia: "The pain in your body flows as a reminder that you are in constant change."

December 25, Croatia: "Even in the pain, there are gifts."

December 28, Croatia: "It does not matter what takes place in these next weeks, months, only that Love is experienced."

December 29, Croatia: "It was here [in Croatia] that I realize I was still feeling angry toward Jonas… his not saying anything in the dance meeting. This was still hanging on."

January 1, Croatia: "I'm hurting as I write this. Alas! Something is still lingering."

January 3, Croatia: "Live in joy, even when there seems to be no joy found. Live in Love, in patience… All around you will go through their own experience. Yours is to be in a place of allowing Love to flow through you."

Chapter 27

Walking Through Gardens

Over the months I thought I had "forgiven" the hurts. And then I realized that *recognizing the anger and sadness* that had surfaced during Christmas was only part of the picture. *Resolving* these deep feelings was a different issue altogether.

I had done nothing but pray and consciously choose to see and come from love, as best I could… asking over and over "Jesus, what would you do? Sai Baba? Gandhi? Buddha?… and anyone else that I knew who would choose a road of love to deal with all the negative thrown at them.

There have been less than a half dozen times in my adult life where I've been visited in the dreamtime by Mother Teresa. It was well into the second year since the incident at Jonas and Sarah's that I can remember her coming, once again, linking her arms into mine and asking me to walk with her into a beautiful garden. I never could actually hear her voice or remember the words she would say to me as we walked. I do recall vividly waking up and understanding clearly that whatever my circumstances, including those that had occurred in Jonas and Sarah's community, my only clear choice was to come from love at all times, and then trust.

Shortly after the last dream where I was visited by Mother Teresa, I came across this quote of St. Teresa that to this day I carry with me wherever I go:

"Let nothing perturb you,
Nothing frighten you.
All things pass. God does not change.
Patience achieves everything."

And so I continued to choose this perspective while being very aware that having confessed so strongly my anger, my choice to come from love was a challenge. Not because I was interested in hanging onto the anger, but because no matter how well intentioned I was, the gnawing feeling of incompleteness hung on… relentlessly. But I didn't give up. I kept praying, day in and day out.

I wrote an insight into my journal:,

"When the way seems unclear, even 'muddy,'
look closely at the mud, become as a child.
Feel it between your toes and make 'play' of it.
Be in the innocence of it all. Then Truth reveals itself."

The final pieces of the experience were falling into place. So much had healed in my soul over the months. I was exhausted and my body, too, had walked such a painful journey. I found myself wanting to utterly surrender, thinking of the thought from the Bible, "Ye who are heavy laden, lay down your burden."

On a winter morning, in my journal I wrote, "Last night I was haunted again by the ghosts of what had taken place at Jonas and Sarah's.. I'm trying to give it all to you, Spirit, yet something keeps hanging onto me. I find I'm still unresolved in regard to it all. I don't know what to do or how to be."

On the same day, I received an insight that this journey for Jonas and Sarah was an important one. That I was being asked to see them as innocent and trust that the land they were on was healing them and all who walked on it. All the while, I am to have faith that all was working together for good.

It reminded me of a similar insight I had received in Bosnia, where it seemed the lush beauty of the plant life and vibrant colors present through the flowers were all helping to heal all that had gone on before. It was in late spring. I have a vivid memory of walking down a dirt road in the countryside outside a small Bosnian village, relishing in the extraordinary wonder and beauty around me shining through the trees and plants. Suddenly, I thought I heard a voice coming from an apple tree as I walked passed, "You don't think you're the only ones called here to help the land and people heal, do you?" I remember laughing and feeling a sense of relief and camaraderie.

The stage was being set for the possibility of a miracle.

Part VI

GRACE

"Stay still in the pain,
rooted in that which is light in you.
Let the sword go through you.
Maybe it is not a sword at all.
Maybe it is a tuning fork.
You become a tone.
You become the music you always
longed to hear.
You did not know you were a song."

— Ylva Eggehorn,
Swedish Poet

Chapter 28

Insights

Being able to identify the anger and subsequently the great sadness I had felt and finding the willingness to admit and express it all out loud was huge for me. It gave me the courage to take a stand — a stand for myself and the choices I had made leading up to the incident that occurred so many months ago.
I look back over my life and find I am deeply grateful to my parents for having raised me in an environment where it was okay, indeed encouraged, to speak openly about my thoughts and feelings, without fear of being judged. As a result I gained confidence and belief in myself. I wasn't very shy in most circumstances. Yet, during much of my life there have been those who have perceived my confidence and curiosity as arrogance and ego. This has caused me over the years to withdraw and hold back at times, from the simple fear of being misunderstood or ostracized. Is this why I waited seven years to share the vision I had been given of a global ceremonial dance? Maybe.

I also was taught to balance my curiosity and confidence with love and to make an effort to understand. I had perfect role models in my parents. I have to admit, however, it hasn't always been easy to juggle my passion to share an idea with the humility and patience necessary to communicate my thoughts or feelings in a way that they could be heard by others. This latter piece has been an ongoing struggle for me. It has been hard knowing since childhood that my destiny lay in the global arena in some way (though I didn't really know how that would play out), and learning early on that this was not a safe topic to discuss beyond a limited few.

What I did know even as a child was that *love* is the crux of everything. Yes, I received love in my family as a child but I'm also clear that I came into this world with a *knowing* about love that is beyond a single lifetime. Perhaps we all do and it is the circumstances one is born into that determines the eventual outcome of one's outlook on life. In my case, I eventually arrived at the conclusion that no matter what, *love will always be the ultimate answer.*

At one point I wrote, "Last night, watching the movie *Elizabeth I* with John, I came to a realization. In those moments, watching young Queen Elizabeth make hard choices and doing the best she could with so much going against her, I felt a kinship with her and to anyone else who has ever had to make choices demanding the best they have to give, knowing there may be challenges and even threats to what one knows to be true. Regarding the *youth dance* of months before, whatever beliefs and experiences others might have had, I, to this day, gently but firmly stand in the truth of the decisions I made at that time. They were made in humility, honesty, with sincere moment by moment prayer for divine guidance, and a deep love for all present."

I'm certain more truths will reveal themselves in time. For now, just knowing this piece has given me strength to trust that all is going to be resolved in a good way, in time.

Chapter 29

Forgiveness

In early February I was taken to a world-class osteopath in Germany to have my back and hips examined. After my time in December with the East Indian doctor in South Africa who told me I would heal myself, I became disciplined with daily exercises, including sound meditation, all of which began to show positive results. This concept wasn't new for me, as I had gone through a journey with cancer some years back and chose at that time to use an alternative route of healing. I relied primarily on the use of sound, mental intention and prayer. It was a true success.

Whatever I now brought to the German osteopath's door, it felt that it was only residual of what had existed in the months prior. After a thorough examination, with bright shining eyes, she grinned and said, "There's very little left for me to do here." She continued on to say my body was almost healed. She then showed me where the pain physically began in the muscle and bones. She then taught me how to help myself should it ever happen again.

I didn't miss the fact that my physical body was healing in synchronous rhythm to the healing of my emotional body. I hadn't been able to see this so clearly as in those moments in Germany.

Knowing, and with great relief, appreciating the long journey I had been on in these many months, I was elated to have identified and exposed the hidden feelings around Jonas that I had suppressed. But now, understanding resolution was imperative, another question came. What do I do with the actual energy of the anger, of the sadness, still within me?

All of a sudden, I found myself back at square one. At least it felt that way. I knew instinctively that *forgiveness* was the key, but this was a word that had little meaning if I didn't *feel* it. Sure, I intellectually got the concept. But to embrace fully the *feeling* of its meaning, to internalize it, was different. I remembered those times as a child when I would get in a squabble with my brother or sister. Mom or Dad would step in and ask us each to apologize to the other. I would say "I'm sorry" to appease my parents, but in my heart of hearts, the last thing I felt was "sorry."

And so here, after having come so far, I was once again staring another level of emotion in the face. While still in Germany, I wrote, "I awoke in the night thinking of Jonas and Sarah. I watched my thoughts as they turned negative. So I got up, knelt and prayed for them, the community there and for John and me… willing myself to *choose Love*… And so every second my mind would wander to a negative thought, I said to myself over and over, *choose Love.* After some time passed, I finally fell asleep."

Chapter 30

Love

There's a saying, "Fake it 'til you make it." Maybe in some way this is what I was doing. I would go through the motions until I hopefully and miraculously would arrive at the place of actually feeling what until now felt like "pretending."

I remember something that happened many years ago when my son was thirteen years old. He had this coat. You know, one of those full length trench coats like the one Keanu Reeves wore in the movie, *The Matrix*. My son, John, had painted skulls on it and decorated it, creatively, with metal chains (made from safety pins). Everytime I saw the coat I cringed, and then, of course, the anger would start bubbling up until I lashed out verbally, in a loud voice, that the coat was putting out an image I'm not sure he (nor I!) wanted. I found all kinds of creative ways to verbally express my anger.

Then, one day, before my son got home from school, I took and hid the coat. Needless to say, he was not pleased. The situation, of course, brought forth more verbal volcanic eruptions from both of us. The next morning, I called a psychologist friend of mine and told him what was happening. I could hear him grinning over the phone. He said, "First, Jeanne, you're afraid. That's what is hidden underneath the anger. I want you to try something. The next time the subject of the coat comes up and you feel the anger starting to bubble up, go ahead and shout the words that are coming, however explosive they are. But this time,

I want you to imagine the word 'Love' imprinted on your son's forehead or flashing in front of you in a bright light."

Well, my opportunity came that same afternoon. No sooner had my son walked through the door than he immediately started searching for the coat. When he couldn't find it, he came at me with a bombast of accusations. I gritted my teeth. As I felt my own vitriolic retort coming, I imagined the word "Love" flashing in front of me. I spewed the words out, changing nothing in my usual delivery of verbal attack, except that this time I was doing all through the filter of the word "Love."

Suddenly, there was silence. My son simply looked at me. Then he quietly sat down and said "Maybe it's time I listen to what you have to say, Mom."

I remember that moment with crystal clear clarity. My knees got shaky and I felt my breath heaving in my chest. I looked into my son's eyes and all the fear around this whole subject of the coat was gone. Finally, he and I were able to have a heart to heart talk. It was then that I became aware of the power of the vibration of a single word… in this case "Love."

Chapter 31

Reaching Out

In late February we were in Wales, still with over two months to go before returning to the States. We were due in Norway for the entire month of March. But plans got abruptly changed. I received a message from my daughter, Jenny, saying she was having heart problems. It was a defective mitral valve. She was being told that she might have to undergo surgery. My own heart skipped a few beats when I heard this. I knew immediately that my husband, John, and I were to cancel any events planned for the remainder of February and March and that I was to go to Jenny to be with her for however long it took.

A few days before leaving the UK, I wrote a card to Jonas and Sarah, both of whom seemed to stay on my mind. I thanked them for having been our friends over all these years and in this, having helped me to learn about myself. The card was part of my effort to walk in integrity by reaching out and doing the best I knew how to come from love… however challenging this continued to be.

But when the time came to drop the card in the post box, I couldn't mail it. I was still struggling emotionally. Something was still gnawing inside of me. What? Was it still anger? I guess I thought that once having identified the suppressed feelings I had had for so long, I would find the anger would hopefully resolve itself by simply dissipating over time. That is, as long as I continued to handle the whole situation honorably and with love. Alas! I still had more to learn.

Before leaving Wales, I received an email from Sarah who said she was looking forward to seeing us when we returned. I have to admit neither John nor I wanted to see Sarah or Jonas. Not yet. John still had his own issues to deal with.

And me? I wasn't ready either. I found my gut still knotting up when the subject came up. I simply wanted to stay focused on my upcoming journey with Jenny. Yet, I knew I couldn't avoid what was appearing blatantly in front of me. I already knew I would contact Sarah when I returned, however uncomfortable I felt.

In my journal, this thought came the day we were to leave Wales for the States, *"Always the way is open to you to choose Love. Always there is a way to see beauty and light even when it appears darkness is unfolding. See the darkness as a doorway to light."* And so, as hard as it was, I chose to keep myself open and flexible where Jonas and Sarah and their community were concerned.

I remember feeling a degree of shame, judging myself for not having totally processed through the hurt that still lingered after so many months. Whether or not the hurt at this point was simply residue from the incident at Jonas and Sarah's, in those moments it felt very real and present. I prayed that eventually it would all fall away. Yet even with this awareness, I knew clearly it was important to reach to the community as lovingly as I could, as I had tried to do every step of the way. But it was also important that I allow myself to feel completely the feelings I still had, no matter how deep they went or for how long they remained.

Having left Wales, it was only a few hours before the first challenge came. Arriving into the States, to our surprise we were met by Ted, the one person who months before, had apologized to me for his part in that Saturday incident. His meeting us was a total surprise as we had asked and expected our friend Lonie to pick us up. Neither John nor I had wanted to engage ourselves in any kind of emotional interaction that we thought might occur should we see Sarah, Jonas or anyone else from their community greeting us at the airport. But dear Lonie, not being fully aware of our plight, contacted Sarah whose own schedule wouldn't allow her to come get us. Sarah thoughtfully made arrangements with Ted to fetch us. She, herself, was helping to nurse an elderly friend who was ill.

It was late and we arrived from overseas quite tired. When I saw Ted's warm smile and arms opened to hug, any trepidation I might have had fell away. It was good to see him. For me, it represented the community attempting to heal itself. At a more basic level, it was a true sign on Ted's part to reach out in friendship.

Chapter 32

Heaven

I was to leave for Jenny's in one week. Three days before, Sarah, John and I met at Starbucks, a favorite place. It truly was good to see Sarah, though I had a few butterflies in my stomach that hadn't yet found formation. The first part of the conversation was light and newsy. Then Sarah asked if there was anything John or I still needed to say in regard to what had happened on their land in the meeting that now seemed to have taken place inside another lifetime.

I could feel John cringe as this was the last thing in the world he wanted to happen. I, however, plunged ahead, sharing what came in those moments, being as honest as I could. Sarah did the same. All in all, it was a good clearing. John, though, still had some feelings to work through that would come when ready. For him, now wasn't the time.

Sarah suggested that when I returned from Jenny's perhaps we could spend time with Jonas as well. There was a mutual agreement that that would happen when the time was "right." For now, I appreciated that Sarah had the courage to engage us in this particular conversation. It was a step forward and helped to open the door further to my own healing. My job was to keep "choosing Love," whatever unresolved pieces were floating around in my psyche.

I arrived in Seattle at eleven thirty in the morning. There, waiting with a glorious smile and a great bear hug, was Jenny. In that instant, I felt the weight of all the many months lift. I was able to breathe and appreciate where I had been and where I was now heading.

How perfect was it that from the gate we walked to a Starbucks there in the terminal. There we met a friend of Jenny's where we celebrated my arrival with our favorite coffee drinks. For me, it was a caramel frappacino, hold the whip cream. Yum! I was in heaven. What a great way to start this special time with my daughter.

On the way from the airport to Jenny's apartment on Puget Sound, we stopped to take a short walk on a nearby rocky beach. It was incredibly beautiful, particularly when the wind carried the waves of the Pacific Ocean high into the air, touching everything within reach with a soft silver mist. In the distance was Mt. Rainier, looming up from the earth to a towering fourteen thousand feet, a sight that takes your breath away. Afterward we went on to Jenny's apartment which faced out onto the Sound.

As we walked through the front door, a sudden torrent of wind, rain and hail, all moving at a high velocity, came sweeping in from the sea. It may be my imagination but it almost felt like a greeting. Wow! I gulped. The adventure at Jenny's was already starting.

Chapter 33

Heart Dance

In the days that followed, together Jenny and I prepared the space in her one-bedroom apartment for my stay, which we both understood could be for a number of weeks or months, should surgery be imminent. Very quickly I found myself adjusting to the role of *serving* my daughter.

I remember the feeling. It was one of relief, of freedom, of anticipation and joy. It was so simple. I was to focus on nothing but service to my child… service filled with pure love, devoid of judgment or second guessing. And after all the years of multitasking, which included constant travel and no permanent physical home, this literally felt like a divine gift.

Five days after my arrival, we were on our way to Portland, Oregon where Jenny was to receive an ultrasound test. It was the start of an ongoing parade of tests and examinations that would lead to the final decision that heart surgery was the wisest choice. It was not an easy choice. She was young. Thirty-six. And to anyone who saw her she radiated health and vitality.

On top of all, Jenny had a track record of having healed herself of other severe ailments in the past. The situation now, however, with her heart, seemed to demand of her a surrender and trust at a level not easy for her… nor for her mother.

Jenny was a commercial pilot for a major airline. With the oncoming possibility of heart surgery she was already preparing for the long days ahead when she would be on disability, going through that time-space tunnel of waiting until the moment she could fly again.

Our days were filled with walks, talks, movies, visiting of her pilot friends, and just simply the joy of living and becoming "reacquainted" with each other. We had not spent so much concentrated time together since her highschool days. It was fun too, getting to know her boyfriend at the time, Cody (also a pilot), and her little rabbit "Gracie," a constant and comforting companion in the small apartment.

Though the days were full and rich, hanging over us was the "surgery cloud" which had taken on new dimensions as the quest for the *right* surgeon began. Jenny made the decision to have robotic surgery done rather than going through the ordeal of having her sternum cracked open only to be followed by many months of healing. The search then for a surgeon became narrowed and simple, particularly as there were to date only a handful of surgeons anywhere in the world capable of doing robotic heart surgery.

As the fates would have it, one of the best surgeons in our country happened to be within thirty minutes of Jenny's apartment.

Once the decision was made, all else seemed to fall into place quickly. The date was set for May 13.

During the weeks that led up to the May date, thanks to my husband John's efforts, people from all over the world were sending prayers. Prayers were coming from Israel, Croatia, South Africa, Australia, and all over Europe and the United States. Jenny received phone calls and emails from friends around the globe assuring her that she was being supported. At times it was a little overwhelming for her, but I could tell it was all touching her deeply, often to the point of tears.

Over the next days and weeks, I shared with Jenny the teachings I had received along the way, teaching her skills and techniques to enhance her own healing process. She, in the meantime, had fragile moments when the reality of the thin veil between life and death set in. I look back on those moments and realize how even in her fragility, she was amazingly brave and wise beyond her years. In those instances, I knew beyond any doubt she was doing the "heart dance" not only for herself but for all of us.

Chapter 34

Wings of Angels

Through the weeks and months, every time the situation with Jonas and Sarah arose in my mind, I prayed for help and sent love through the ethers. With Mt. Rainier soaring into the skies, so close it seemed as though you could reach out and touch it, and with the sight of Mt. Saint Helens and Mt. Hood filling us with a sense of awe each time we passed by on our way to Jenny's cardiologist in Portland, my ongoing under-the-surface thought of Jonas and Sarah found blessed perspective. My focus was on serving Jenny. Nothing else. My job was loving what or who was in front of me in that moment, and in this case, it was Jenny. I trusted God would take care of everything else.

It was a real test for me. And it was made easy in part because of my deep devotion and love for my child.

As the time for Jenny's surgery neared, there was a sense of inevitability taking hold… a knowing that we were at the point of no return. Too much effort had gone into the preparation to turn back now.

Jenny's father Jim, her brother John and his fiancée, Brandy, had arrived the day before her surgery was to take place, to be by her side. It was such a blessing to have them there. They had all traveled across the country to spend these crucial hours with

Jenny. It was wonderful having them all present, and especially so to have my precious son John there.

At one point, Jenny and her brother called me into her bedroom to present me with a Mother's Day gift. It was a ring they had had made, carrying their birthstones with mine centered between the two of theirs. With tears they said, "Now Mom, this will remind you that we are always with you no matter where you are in the world." What they didn't know is that it was the two of them I would often see in my dreams, standing beside me, one on each side, supporting me always when I seemed to need it most. Once again I thought of the incident at Jonas and Sarah's.

Jenny's boyfriend Cody and I drove Jenny to the hospital early that Wednesday morning. Her father, brother, and his fiancée were to follow shortly after. I found myself becoming teary knowing that prayers from all over the world were being sung and spoken for my daughter. In those early moments I received a flash of understanding of what it means to be carried on the *wings of angels.*

The first hours passed in a mist of surrealism. Here I was, with Jenny's father, my son John and his soon-to-be wife, Brandy, in a container of love whose sole purpose was to support Jenny, to be there for her physically, emotionally and spiritually.

The actual hours that Jenny was in surgery moved in slow motion for me. I half expected my own voice to come out in a movie rendition of the sluggish distorted effect of slow-motion sound.

In one respect, the few hours with my son and the others were a gift — we had such rare moments together. Jim and I were able to catch up a bit, reminiscing some humorous memories here and there. It was especially wonderful to have these concentrated moments with my son John and Brandy. Then there was Cody, Jenny's boyfriend, whose love and care of her was something that to this day touches my heart.

The surgery turned out to be a great success. Jenny successfully transcended the hurdle that had been placed in front of her, thanks to her own strength and courage, and to all who came to her aid. This included the surgeon, and his whole medical staff. Jenny and I both were convinced a team of *angels* had shown up to help her, disguised as nurses and other staff members of the hospital.

Now, the journey to recovery had begun. And as with most journeys, there were some surprises in store.

Chapter 35

Realization

After an extended and much needed stay in the hospital, Jenny came home with a determination that would inspire anyone to reach for the stars, knowing beyond any doubt, the stars are truly attainable.

Each day, right from the start, Jenny began walking to strengthen her heart, first in small increments of five minutes or less. Within two weeks she was walking thirty minutes a day. And by the end of a month she was up to fifty minutes a day.

Day by day she grew stronger. It was pure joy being with her. And I have to admit that cooking her meals and serving her in a way that helped to make her life easier while she was on this journey, fed my soul as much as it did hers.

One morning I awoke with Jonas and Sarah heavy on my mind. I realized that in these past weeks, allowing myself the gift of focusing so completely on Jenny, I had, by choice except in fleeting moments, not thought about them and all that had occurred months earlier. This had been the right thing to do. Because what I didn't see until some time later was that I, too, was healing. Something inside me was opening up, something that I realized had closed off after the Saturday incident. At the same time, I was aware of a subtle persistent feeling that wouldn't let me go… a constant whispering that not all was complete here.

I found I continued to carry a great sadness in my heart toward Jonas and Sarah. I prayed for help. I thought that in these weeks with Jenny, I would have finally resolved all that had happened in that Saturday dance meeting. Apparently not yet.

So I asked myself, with tears and passion, what was it that I needed to resolve this *once and for all*?!? Some might say "Just forget it. Get a hold of yourself, and simply empty your mind of the whole ordeal, and walk away!" This might work for some but even for those who make this choice, it doesn't resolve the actual issue or take care of the energy that remains trapped in the cells of one's body and psyche.

It took a while for me to reach hard and deep inside my soul. FINALLY! One early morning I heard a voice ask me, *"What do you want? What are you needing?"* Without hesitancy, I blurted out, *"I NEED TO HEAR JONAS SAY 'I'M SORRY!"* There it was! It was so simple. This was the nagging piece that would not let me go. The piece that hid in the dark until now. After all this time, after all the work and care that had gone into the healing of the whole situation surrounding the incident of so many months prior, this piece had remained completely and absolutely elusive.

Once I recognized and acknowledged my need for an apology, I found myself asking the questions "Okay, should, by some remote chance, you receive an apology, *what then*? Is your life and the road ahead truly dependent on the acts of another? And what if Jonas cannot apologize or doesn't see any reason why he should, *what then*?" So many questions began popping up in my mind.

Here is what I knew. Something my dad taught me. No matter how hard you may try, you can't know all that is going on inside another person's mind. There are those I'm sure that would argue. But the reality was I had no idea what had gone on for Jonas, or for anyone else for that matter, in regard to that Saturday dance meeting. I could surmise and speculate but all I knew for certain was that something had taken place then that was so painful that its experience left layers of debris that took months to wade through, as I tried to make any sense of it all.

For myself I knew that I was the only one who had control over the choices *I* made. I chose to feel the hurt, not to ignore it. I chose to see through love's eyes even when the anger began to surface. I chose to consciously move through the whole experience with fully opened eyes, breathing the entire way. And when I look back on it all, I think I was able to make these choices because I knew getting stuck in the pain was not an option. I trusted and knew that sooner or later *resolve* would come. My hope was that it would be a loving one, and that it would come soon.

The truth was I realized the chances of Jonas' apologizing to me were very slim, particularly as I suspected he nor Sarah were even aware of what had fully happened in that spring meeting on their land. If this were true, *what then*?

Chapter 36

Keeping Time

In the wee hours one morning I walked through a variety of mental images in my mind. At one point, I imagined that I was the one saying "I'm sorry" to Jonas, Sarah and all. Then, with a jolt, I realized that the only thing I was truly sorry for was being a part, consciously or otherwise, of some dynamic that had occurred on that one Saturday that created a space for hurt to happen. It was an uncomfortable feeling and almost seemed unhealable.

Flashes of Bosnia flitted across my mind. Had I come to a dead end? Had I gone as far as I could, only to arrive at an impasse? Had the journey from Bosnia to here been a futile one? Was the answer, "Live with it. Tough it out! Suck it up! You might as well. There's no hope that any true resolve can happen here, other than simply letting time pass, erasing, stamping out, suppressing the hurt that eventually knots up in the soul like a cancerous tumor. After all, this is the fiber of which our human history on this planet is made."

I began to get an inkling of what *hopelessness* meant. I wondered if so many who had survived the kind of tragedy that occurred in the Bosnian war, reached a point in their own healing process beyond which they seemed not to be able to go.

If I really had gone as far as I, myself, could go in regard to my quest in finding an answer to how healing happens after such profound hurt has been experienced, I imagined I could live with that. But, it would be like living with a massive thorn in my side. I would always wonder if complete and total healing was even possible, outside of a miracle.

Miracle! Hmmmm…

In the deepest part of me, I knew nothing was "unhealable." I didn't know what the answer was, except that I was certain the key was *Love.* I knew it would take patience and with patience would come wisdom. I just had to ask myself, "Am I strong enough?"

When I've looked back at the journey Jenny was taking with her heart, I'm interested that the healing of my own heart was "keeping time" with her odyssey. How was this happening?

I don't pretend to understand it all but I have a sneaking suspicion that we are each so interconnected that *when one person heals it makes it possible for another to heal,* even if the two are on opposite ends of the earth. That's what I mean when I say Jenny was doing the "heart dance" for all of us. Maybe we do this for each other everyday but are not aware of the impact our own experiences have on others.

Chapter 37

Suspension

The last Sunday in May Jenny and I decided to go see the new movie, "Star Trek." The theater was packed. Our seats were in the very center of the auditorium. We were surrounded on all four sides by excited trekkies. There was a hush of anticipation as the music began and the first visuals came onto the screen. Everyone sat totally still, absorbed in the opening scenes. Suddenly Jenny's head fell over on my shoulder. Then she abruptly jumped up out of her seat and began running over the people in our row to get out. Apologizing profusely as I tripped over dozens of feet to get to Jenny, I found her sitting on a bench in the lobby. She was in a cold sweat and white as a ghost. Knowing that seconds can make a difference when dealing with the possibility of heart failure, I asked the theater personnel to call 911.

In three minutes, the paramedics showed up. I was deeply grateful, astounded and impressed by the proficiency of the crew and the speed of their arrival. They put Jenny through a series of quick tests and concluded she needed to be taken to the hospital's emergency room. They took her directly to the hospital where she had had her surgery.

Further tests were done, which included x-rays and an echo-cardiogram. Once all was said and done, the results were puzzling. Jenny's heart was showing evidence of leakage. A valve was not closing completely. The blood was being pumped through the heart and there was a possibility of blood backing up into the lungs.

Once again, we were in a state of suspension, having more questions than there were answers. The main and immediate concern was that she might have to undergo another operation.

Jenny was monitored twenty-four hours a day. Each day the medical staff assessed her situation, and after a week the prospect of further surgery was still in question. Jenny wasn't out of hot water yet.

Daily living in a surreal suspension, Jenny was watched over carefully for thirty days. There were more tests accompanied with the ongoing "waiting game." This stretched from days into weeks into months. The amazing thing was Jenny herself and her ability to transcend the moment and shine light wherever she went. At one point, I remember one early morning hearing her laughing, deep rich laughter. I started laughing in response, out of the sheer joy of hearing her.

Who was it that said, "There's nothing so serious that it can't be laughed at." Whatever was happening, choices at a soul level were being made here. Rather than falling into a depression over her situation which would have been understandable, Jenny was rising above her circumstances. She was consciously choosing to see with different eyes. She was choosing love instead of fear. As was said earlier, it doesn't mean she didn't have her moments of insecurity, but those were few, and the choice to deal with all positively, gave her strength and opened her up for insight.

It was during this time that I allowed myself to let the unresolved issue with Jonas and Sarah fully surface. In my journaling I kept getting that my only choice was *unconditional love.* Not knowing how to do this other than to say and pray the words, I kept choosing to see Jonas, Sarah and their community in light, sending out, as best I could, vibrations of love. Then, I simply had to trust.

In the meantime, my focus was to continue to be on Jenny, serving her in as nurturing a way as possible.

Chapter 38

Trust

On June 12, I wrote into my journal:

Careful of letting yourself get caught in the quagmire of emotions that flow when birth is taking place.

Be at peace with yourself and trust all is okay.
See only beauty here.
Be in love with life.

That night I slept very little. I spent hours tossing and turning, thinking and agonizing over all that had transpired at Jonas and Sarah's, paralyzed in thought, astounded to think that the fangs of that one Saturday's event so many months ago would still have such a strong hold on me. "Damn!!" I thought. "Will I ever be done with this? Just when I think the last piece is resolved, something else comes crashing to the surface!"

The feeling of mistrust around Jonas loomed over me like a giant flashing neon sign. I confirmed what I knew about Jonas. I had never questioned his heart. I did question his sense of judgment, particularly in regard to me. I found that no matter how often I felt I had released the hurt and anger, it always seemed to reappear again at some later date. I was truly struggling with this and was screaming for help.

I kept reexamining myself… daily it seemed. And now, somehow, I knew I had reached the final straw. I went over and over anything I might have said or done that would have provoked the kind of harsh dismantling that had occurred at

Jonas and Sarah's. I walked back through the months following the Saturday incident. After thorough and harsh self examination, I kept arriving at the same conclusion: at no time did I come from anything but love for the people in my prayers and in my actions. My dear husband remains a credible witness to this.

On June 13, I recorded in my journal much of the mental struggle I was going through: "I believe I have acted in an honorable way. But I also know something continues asking for resolve and I don't know how to give it or attain it. I want with all my heart to walk with integrity. So, God, how do I do that while I'm eating away inside?…"

My own experience, as well as John's, is that neither Jonas, Sarah, nor most in their community saw the truth of what actually occurred. And because I was quite ill at the time of the meeting on that critical Saturday, I didn't have the strength then to communicate clearly. I was judged with insufficient, incomplete and/or incorrect information and realized in the end, as Sarah had later shared, it had been a *witch hunt.*

Strange. I began to have a real sense of what those in the Bosnian war might have experienced in trying to reconcile what occurred between neighbors who had grown up side by side and who then, in the war, ended up torturing each other. It was a madness. It was *insanity.*

And so… How does one forgive?

Chapter 39

Memory

You know the feeling you have when something or someone is trying to find you, but you're not sure what or who that someone is? It was a bit like that. It was only when I managed to get perfectly still inside that a particular word started surfacing. The word was *grace.* Grace.

I looked the word grace up in the Merriam-Webster's Dictionary. The first definition for this word is: "Unmerited divine assistance given to humans for their regeneration of sanctification; a virtue coming from God; a state of sanctification [purification] enjoyed through divine grace."

Then I received the following words in my journaling on June 13:

The fruit is not ready to fall from the tree yet, but soon it will be. Healing is not far away.

Be patient with yourself. Be gentle.

Much is Happening unseen… Much is occurring at a level that doesn't reveal itself right now but will in time.

Be loving in all your ways.

See Jonas and Sarah, the whole community, in Love's light, and in this you will find healing for yourself.

It was on a Sunday morning when I received a telephone call from my dear friend, Sammye Jo Harvey. She was calling from Germany. Sammye is Native American of the Chippewa Nation. She called to share something she had seen in ceremony that was confirming why it was important that I was there with Jenny. She had seen Jenny in another time, being cut and ripped from my womb in a violent act, tearing her with cruel force from me. My only concern was for Jenny, none for myself. I, apparently, in the moment of violence, was terrified thinking of what Jenny must have been going through as she was being torn from my body. Sammye shared that Jenny's and my time together now was to heal from all that had happened in that other time.

The odd thing is that as Sammye was sharing her insights, I became acutely aware that what had happened at Jonas and Sarah's produced similar feelings as to what I might have experienced in the scenario Sammye was describing: a literal wrenching of my gut! Just as Jenny had been torn from me in another time, my experience at Jonas and Sarah's was one of having my child, in this case, *the dance* to which I'd given birth, being torn from me before it had a chance to stand fully on its own!

This became blatantly clear when I dreamed, the night after that eventful Saturday, of the spirit of the dance crying out, *"Mother, don't let them molest me!"*

Chapter 40

Grace

Inside books I read, I often mark places with bits and pieces of paper with something written on them that have special meaning for me. On this one particular day in June while still at Jenny's this one quote fell into my lap:

There comes a time when all the cosmic tumblers have clicked into place and the Universe opens itself up to see what is possible.

— from the movie, Field of Dreams

As these thoughts flooded over me, I saw another missing piece of the puzzle falling into place. I was suddenly aware that everything that I had gone through, all the months that followed that Saturday meeting at Jonas and Sarah's, seemed to be coming to some sort of climax. Details of the whole experience were surfacing en mass! I, through sheer will, knew instinctively that it was crucial to breathe and stay centered. Each minute that passed was an island unto itself… whole, alive, and pulsating within my awareness.

My time in Washington was coming to an end. Jenny, even with the new developments around her heart, was so much stronger. She was venturing out, already testing her newfound wings. It was time to let her leap from the nest that had held her and nurtured her over these past weeks.

I became teary at times, not wanting to leave, though knowing it was almost time to go. And I guess, at some level, maybe selfishly, I didn't want to leave just yet because I was hoping my personal struggle to heal in the situation with Jonas and Sarah would happen before I actually had to depart.

Then, one morning of the last week at Jenny's, I realized with absolute certainty that it was time to move on. If anything more was to occur during my time in Washington around the incident at Jonas and Sarah's, now was the time. All the cosmic tumblers had fallen into place.

And, indeed, something did happen. Something I would remember for the rest of my life. I might have missed it had all the prior weeks and months of anguish and prayer not prepared me for that one moment when the heavens opened up to give a gift that changed my life forever.

It happened this way…

One day before Jenny's birthday in mid-June, we took a day trip to a part of the ocean where the beaches ran for miles, virtually unpopulated except for the majestic seagulls in constant flight.

It was late in the afternoon, the time of day where the sun is in the first stages of setting, coloring the sky with an assortment of red, pink and purple hues. There was a storm way in the distance playing off the sea's horizon with its dramatic clouds of dark blue and silver. And as so often happens, the sun peeked through the clouds to spray its light in fanlike rays onto the water creating a majestic yet surreal panorama.

The ocean's waves were as dramatically beautiful as the sun's performance. They were rich, high and seemed anxious to roll to shore. And over the water was a thin veil of mist draped gently and as elegantly as a fragile lace lightly touching the dancing waves.

I was standing in the water, in bare feet, letting the wind sing through my hair as the waves wrapped around my feet. Jenny was in her own reverie some one hundred yards or so down the beach. I was alone. My senses were heightened with no conscious effort on my part. Maybe it was the beauty I was seeing. It seemed to permeate every cell of my body.

Suddenly, the water, together with the sun, did something I've only experienced twice in my waking life and once in the dreamtime. A dynamic was created where the water and the sun became a single entity, a single force. And then a light came, a light so brilliant that all I could do was allow the miracle of the moment to come into me, into my soul… changing me, lifting me, healing me.

It all happened in the split of a second. *Grace! Grace*, that mysterious experience that can only be described as holy… touched me! Some would call it *the divine breath of God.*

I stood silent and still as the water playfully pulled the sand from underneath my feet. I didn't realize it at the time, but I was in a state of *ecstasy,* a state of heightened awareness. Time was irrelevant. I could have been there for hours or only seconds. It didn't matter. Something beyond my ordinary state of reality had taken place.

When I regained my equilibrium, I sang a prayer of gratitude knowing something profound had just occurred. It was in those moments that a fleeting thought of Jonas flew through my mind. As it did, I took a breath and hit the reverse button. I replayed the Jonas tape. I played it over and over again to be certain of what I was feeling. There was no more emotional "push-pull," no more knotting up in my belly, no more struggling.

I searched in every nook and cranny of my being to see if I was missing something, making sure there wasn't a hidden rogue feeling or thought lurking in the dark places of my heart or mind ready to pounce on me when I least expected it. Nope! There was nothing! Only light!

I took another deep breath. This was real! The proverbial coiled rubber band that I had let bind my soul over all these months had at last come to rest.

With tears, I backed out of the water and walked toward Jenny. The sun had now disappeared below the horizon. It was time to go.

In those few moments at the ocean's edge, I had stepped into a gentler reality, where all was resolved in a flash of light… as though a karmic balance had been met. I had found a peace deep within me.

I have to admit this feeling felt a bit fragile at first, but this was only because it was so new. And for now, I would walk lightly around my newfound freedom.

Part VII

COMING FULL CIRCLE

"Out beyond ideas of right-doing and wrong-doing,
there is a field.
I will meet you there."

— Rumi

Chapter 41

Resolve

The day before I was to leave Jenny's, flying back to the arms of my husband John and all that waited there, I woke up thinking once again of Jonas and Sarah. They lived a short distance from where John and I would be staying. I wondered what it would be like when we saw each other again. What words would pass between us? I prayed, as I had so many times over the last year, that whatever happened, may I speak and act only from love. A voice inside me asked "what is it that you want?" I said outloud, "I want to move on." Another question came, "What needs to happen to make this possible?"

All at once, I saw it. It was clear. I knew what I would say when I first saw Jonas and Sarah. I would ask their forgiveness, particularly of Jonas… forgiveness for having carried such harsh and angry thoughts toward him over the many months. And though I had, at times, had similar feelings toward Sarah, I never felt she was the pivotal point around which decisions had been made that brought so many and so much into a spiraling vortex of painful change.

In retrospect, I know it was all perfect. The event where I experienced Jonas and his community turning on me, created a stage where each player on it could look deep within themselves if they chose… where each of us was given an opportunity to make a choice that would either catapult the individual into a higher state of being and awareness or would keep her/himself in a state of pseudo-euphoria and denial, pretending that what really happened didn't happen. Whatever the choice, something of immense magnitude and possibility had taken place. And now, having come so far, the journey for me was coming to closure. I was making the choice to move on with the final step… asking Jonas's forgiveness.

In my journal I wrote, "Keep your eyes on Me." This came from a time several years ago when I had been diagnosed with cancer and at one point, found myself slipping into unconsciousness. I was sliding into an unknown space and I was afraid. My eyes happened to fall on an image of Jesus that was in the room. All at once, I was hearing, "Keep your eyes on Me." Repeatedly this comforting message kept coming as I drifted into darkness. And here, once again the message was coming, "Keep your eyes on Me."

These were the words I kept repeating to myself when two days after arriving from Jenny's, I was sitting in a favorite Chinese Restaurant waiting to have dinner with Jonas and Sarah. I was nervous, yet, I knew, beyond any doubt, that I had done the right thing in calling Sarah immediately after my return.

I was grateful that both she and Jonas were open to our having dinner. Chinese was always a good choice, having shared many laughs over prior meals of oriental delicacies and hot tea.

The day of our dinner date, John was running a fever and was coming down with a cold. He chose to let me go alone. At first, I was upset at not having my "brave knight" beside me. It turned out, however, that it couldn't have been more perfect.

Driving to the restaurant I reflected on an Arabic tradition of reconciliation that John and I learned in our travels. It is called *Sulha.* When two tribes or families have been in conflict, reconciliation can begin when the head of one family invites the head of the other to share in a cup of tea. If the one invited chooses to turn down the invitation then reconciliation won't happen… at least, not yet. When the time comes that the invitation is accepted, then the next step occurs when an actual cup of tea is offered. If the invited guest refuses to drink, then again, reconciliation will not happen, not at that time. It is when finally the invited tribal leader not only accepts the invitation of the other Chief but chooses to drink tea he has been offered, that the terms of reconciliation can begin. An interesting custom.

I got to the restaurant to find Jonas and Sarah had not yet arrived. I was greeted by a familiar and friendly face. Linda was a waitress who had waited on John and me many times and, over time, endeared herself to both of us. Upon seeing me, she gave a warm smile and welcome and immediately led me to John's and my favorite booth. She then disappeared only to return a few seconds later with a pot of hot tea. I smiled, thinking of *Sulha.*

As I sat at our table waiting for Jonas and Sarah to appear, I gingerly laid out next to me the gifts I had brought for them. One was a bottle filled with water from the Pacific Ocean. This was for Sarah, who had an affinity for water and its healing qualities. For Jonas I had gathered fresh cedar from the Northwest, to be used however he wanted… in his inipis (sweat lodges) or elsewhere. And the final gift was the card I had written weeks before when in Wales but couldn't bring myself to mail at the time, the card that carried my words of gratitude for their having been John's and my friends for so many years.

I pondered over these simple gifts. I planned in my mind that the dinner that night would consist of three pieces. After the initial greetings, 1) I would ask forgiveness of Jonas, for having carried for so long, feelings of anger, however justified I might have thought they were at one time; 2) I would give Jonas and Sarah their gifts; and 3) we then would spend the rest of dinner laughing and sharing light conversation. There would be no need to rehash all that had happened on that long-past Saturday afternoon.

I've never known who it was that said "If you want to make God laugh, make a plan." Whoever it was, grasped an insightful reality.

When Jonas and Sarah walked into the restaurant, I found the nervousness dissolving like a thin vapor, feeling my heart respond at the sight of them with deep affection.

As soon as we gave our food order to Linda, I turned to Jonas and shared that there was something I needed to say to him. It was then I asked his forgiveness. Jonas asked, "Forgiveness for what?" I explained. As gingerly as possible, I walked back over the months, describing the rollercoaster ride of emotions I had endured in an attempt to make sense of all that had taken place in that Saturday meeting on their land. I was very conscious of not wanting to go into too much detail, because I felt it unnecessary. My focus was clear. I was there to heal a broken relationship, to ask Jonas' forgiveness for anger I had felt toward him, and to create a bridge so that moving forward was possible for each of us.

My explanation, no matter how well intentioned, prompted Jonas to ask more questions and before I knew it, we were into a full-blown conversation over all that had happened so many months before, the very thing I didn't want to do. It felt like some gigantic force was pulling each of us into a replay of what had taken place that critical weekend.

It became clear that my suspicions had been on target. Neither Jonas nor Sarah, particularly Jonas, seemed to understand the fullness of what had occurred that memorable Saturday. And now? It didn't matter. Had this conversation taken place even two weeks before, I might have felt an emotional charge around the whole topic that was surfacing now. But because of my experience at the ocean, I found I could be in this conversation with these old friends and feel only love for them.

And so, for three hours, we "broke bread," drank tea and shared from our hearts. At some deep level, reconciliation was happening, the friendship was being restored.

It was somewhere toward the end of our time together that I noticed a golden glow had settled over our table. We were engulfed in a radiance that brought with it, a prophetic insight. I was urged to pull above and notice what was happening. It was the deep-seated understanding that if we (Jonas, Sarah and I) could truly heal from all that had gone before, then the possibility for a world to do the same had opened up.

It was a confirmation again that if any one of us can heal completely, it makes it possible for all of us, a whole world, to heal.

Suddenly, I saw with blinding awareness answers to the questions born from my time in Bosnia, questions that had haunted and tormented me: *How was the horror of betrayal from those one has so deeply trusted, even possible? And how, then, do relationships (friends, relatives, countries) so split apart, heal?* The answers that came through the journey that began on an innocent spring Saturday are embedded in my soul for eternity.

I had walked my own journey through hell with anguish and heartbreak, and with a determination to consistently bring *love* into the equation. As a result, the miracle of *Grace* had taken place. Forever, my world had changed.

Part VIII

EPILOGUE

"There is no separation.
Only differences that emphasize the beauty
of the many facets of Love."

— Jeanne White Eagle

Epilogue

December, 2011

Time really is a funny thing. If one waits long enough, the reality of an experience takes on new perspective. I wonder if that is because the event itself at the moment it is happening, sets into motion a direction for the *psyche* that is quite different from one that might have been, had the incident never occurred. I can hear one of my children say, "Well duh, Mom?!?! Isn't that the way it always happens?" A person goes along in a particular direction, however noble or mundane, only to find that in a nano-second everything changes and suddenly the new set of circumstances causes us to shift perspective. In an instant, our lives are changed forever. This certainly is the case for someone who finds her or his life quickly turned upside-down when an earthquake or tsunami hits with little warning.

And so, I guess you might say that is what happened to me at Jonas and Sarah's. For me, an *earthquake* of the highest category. And I ask the reader's forgiveness if this may seem an exaggeration. But I realize, in looking back now with some distance in time, any incident that brings a person face to face with the truth of who he or she is, testing all one's values and belief systems with ultimate abandon and force, the experience itself shakes up and rearranges the foundation of who one supposed her/himself to be. Oddly, it is not a *thinking* process. If it were, who in their "right mind" would choose such torture for themselves? Certainly, an abused child doesn't have such luxury.

Nor, does it seem, do vulnerable recipients of war games or natural disaster.

For myself, I find I have come through these last years and months having grown stronger, much wiser and more patient. I look back and feel a certain humble satisfaction in knowing I truly acted in the highest way I knew at the time. And to be honest, I'm not sure I would handle anything differently now were I presented with the same situation. My prayer is, however, that I don't have to experience such pain again, nor would I wish this onto anyone who might have gone through something in their life that hurt them so deeply.

I am interested that since my time following that one fateful Saturday with Jonas and Sarah's community, how aware I've become of others having gone through an experience of deep betrayal of one sort of another, none of which can be measured by anyone's gauge other than that of the person bearing the particular experience itself.

There's the story of a dear friend in Germany, whose own sister betrayed her by refusing her participation in the celebration of a family wedding. Because our friend had chosen a different path in life for herself, one that didn't fit the box that her sister wanted to put her in, she was ostracized. This is a soul whose only intent is to love a world where so much hate exists, whose daily effort is spent in bringing beauty to all she touches.

Another story came from a young white woman, born in South Africa, who as a child was sexually abused by her father. Such betrayal by a parent to a child is the height of brutality one human being can impose upon another. You might say this young woman had every reason to grow up into a bitter and spiteful person. But over the years, this amazing woman consciously chose instead to deal with her situation with love, much because of the love given her by the family's black maid, who, at the time, was living through the brutality of Apartheid. This young woman forgave her father for his abuse of her and an environment that would allow such abuse. She has since found the courage to write a book of poems (now published) telling her story to help others who have gone through similar abuse.

Then there is the story of my own beloved husband, John, who as a child experienced what for him was the betrayal of both parents. Because of his mother's emotional and mental instabilities that had her going in and out of mental hospitals, she was not available for her son's upbringing. Nor was John's father who eventually abandoned his 13 year old son to a "boy's farm." In the very early years, John's memory of family was molded by unwelcomed experiences of abusive environments in a foster home and short sporadic visits with distant relatives. Moving into adult years then brought the challenge of making life choices that were not filled with bitterness and resentment. Though it hasn't been an easy journey for him at times, John has emerged as one of the gentlest and most loving human beings I know.

I could go on and on with the stories of betrayal that have appeared "suddenly" in the last months… of some employers and their uncaring treatment of those who trust and work for them, of couples who have carelessly betrayed each other, tearing at the moral fiber of the family unit, etc. etc. I could also share stories from people who, just like my own experience, believed an old hurt had been dealt with and resolved only to find it surface again and again until *finally* at some point in time, a glorious and absolute *release* came. It is then and only then that healing at the deepest level could take place. Perhaps this is fodder for a new book one day…

As for Jonas and Sarah's community everything changed. Many people left and moved on. Others stayed. And over time new people have come. Though my husband and I are not often in the area any more, we have on occasion shared meals and conversations here and there with those who stayed, and have nurtured and continued contact with Sarah in particular.

For now, all I know is that something within me is different. Colors are more vibrant. Sounds are clearer. And the Love I feel is deeper, gentler and more profound. Life is good.

Acknowledgements

There are extraordinary people who have been a part of bringing *Grace* into being, those without whom this book would most likely have not been written. Each played a unique and important role for me and I wish to acknowledge some of them here. First, I want to thank our dear Croatian, Bosnian and Danish friends, particularly Sanja, Vanja, Dragan and Andreas whose courage, strength and patience were a constant inspiration. Then I wish to thank Jonas, Sarah and their community for giving me the gift of learning more about myself and what I know now to be the lasting and true nature of Love.

When I knew it was time to tell my story, I knew I would need somewhere quiet and nurturing. Three ladies in particular stepped up to the plate. Anne Klanderud in Norway offered to let me stay as long as I wished in her log cabin by a wonderful lake nestled in the picturesque Norwegian hills. Lesley Waldron offered her beautiful log cabin hidden in the quiet Northeast of Rangeley, Maine. Then, Janet Ennis gifted her vacation house in Hoodsport, Washington where every day we were greeted by seagulls, one lone eagle, and playful waves finding their way inland from the Pacific Ocean. These three dear ladies, as well as our close friends Jo Fisher and Ula Rae Mynatt who have housed my husband and me for months at a time, allowed the space and solitude for the birthing of a book to take place.

Thank you profusely to Joe Nusbaum with Eltanin Publishing who in his expert and gentle guidance and advice has made the whole experience of getting *Grace* out of the birthing canal a true pleasure. Kudos also go to Eltanin's staff, in particular, Cathy Ryan, for their skill and patience throughout.

Thank you to all those who stuck their necks out to read *Grace* long before it was ready for publishing and who offered insights and helpful comments along the way. That includes you, Pat Joynes, and your gift of early editing. It includes you, Monty Joynes, Tom Bissinger, Sue Mehrtens, John Renesch and all who are amazing authors in your own right, and others of you who took the time to read *Grace*. There were many of you and I ask your forgiveness for not mentioning all the names here. You know who you are and I hope you also know it has been an honor to have you part of this project.

Thank you to those who have inspired me over the years to always come from a place of Love: my parents Perry Lane and Kit Haynes, Satya Sai Baba, and Joseph Rael in particular. I have been blessed with profound teachers and teachings throughout my life. To name them all would be a feat that would require another book. I'll just say here, Thank You to a loving Universe who has placed extraordinary souls in my path. May each of them be blessed a thousand-fold in blessings.

And then, thank you to my dear husband, John Pehrson, whose patience in allowing me to read aloud long portions of the book again and again to gain his wisdom and instructive criticism, which he happily shared from time to time.

Thank you to my beloved children, Jenny and John Troutner, and my daughter-in-law Brandy, who simply through their love, along with that of my precious husband, gave me strength and the courage to continue down this path of sharing my story of *Grace*. The whole journey has truly been one of profound healing.

About the Author

Jeanne White Eagle (Jeanne Lane Pehrson) is an educator and futurist with Cherokee roots. She is co-author of two books on conflict resolution, a founding member (Cast C) of the international musical "Up With People," worked in the international business arena where she was awarded the prestigious Willis Harman Award by the World Business Academy, and is founder of *Up on the Mountain*, an organization for teens at risk. She is an accomplished composer and professional classical singer.

Skilled in Conflict Resolution techniques, as of 1996 when she was given the name of Jeanne White Eagle by Native American mystic Joseph Rael, she has followed a vision that has taken her husband, John Pehrson, and herself around the world, often into war zones and other areas of deep conflict. With the use of Sound, Movement and the Open Heart Process, a process designed to help resolve conflict, she and her husband have become Ambassadors for worldwide peace. (In 2009, a biography of Jeanne and John was released, called *Journey for the One* by Monty Joynes.)

18395868R00105

Made in the USA
Charleston, SC
01 April 2013